Swimming from A-Z:

Alaska to Zimbabwe

Rick Powers

To JOHN,
Hope you enjoy my
stories. I know you can relate because
of your P.C. experience.
Best wishes,
Rick Feb, 2011

PUBLISH AMERICA

PublishAmerica
Baltimore

ISBN: 978-1-4489-8816-7
PUBLISHED BY PUBLISHAMERICA, LLLP
www.publishamerica.com
Baltimore

Printed in the United States of America

For all my wonderful swimmers whose lives I have touched and who have touched mine.

A special thank you to Meiling Sicam who took the time twice to read and correct the manuscript, Sergio Bulat for his intelligent advice, Nancy Ottum for helping with the covers and numerous former swimmers for their comments on specific chapters they were a part of.
A website with photos to accompany all chapters will be available in March 2010. Contact me at *rpswimmer@hotmail.com* at that time. Rick Powers

Prologue

No, this is not a "how to" swimming book. The swimming community already has many excellent technical books to choose from. I have had a life filled with unique experiences, many related to the fact that for 42 years, from 1966 to 2008, I coached swimming teams in 10 different countries on five continents and gave clinics in 30 countries.

I survived an assassination attempt, irate husbands, crazy swimming parents, an arrest by the FBI, and over the years, discovered that sleaze and corruption is alive and well at all levels in the swimming world.

I approached each new coaching position with the attitude that I could make an impact and contribute to the progress of swimming on a regional or even national level. Often, I was stymied by the old guard of coaches and federation officials who, invariably, feel threatened by the new kid on the block and fear losing face if the newcomer is successful. I fought the good fight for as long as possible, only moving on when it became apparent that I was hitting my head against a brick wall. But swimming, or any sport for that matter, is just a slice of the pie. There is more to life than just the job and I made the most of my time away from the pool, too, as shall become evident to the reader very shortly.

Enjoy my story.

Chapter I
The Peace Corps and Ecuador, 1966-67

Born in the Bronx and raised in Chicago, I began swimming competitively at the South Chicago YMCA at age 11 and competed, with little success, for the next 10 years. Despite a lack of talent, I thoroughly enjoyed the swim team atmosphere, staying in shape, the social advantages of being on the team in college and the camaraderie with my teammates. Approaching graduation at Eastern Illinois University in March 1966, I received a rude awakening. Having dropped an unneeded class in my final semester and, though already having been accepted into graduate school, I had dipped under the required number of units necessary to avoid the military draft. I applied to the Peace Corps, at the time a legal alternative to military service and was accepted only three days before my scheduled physical.

The Peace Corps would prefer that you have a skill useful for service in an underdeveloped country. I had no recognizable skills but I did mention on my application that I had 10 years of competitive swimming experience. Fortunately for me, in its early years, the PC had a sports program. I was assigned, along with some 30 other young people with competitive sports backgrounds, to a three-month summer training camp at Denison University in Ohio. The camp was fun. We had the university to ourselves. There were no other students on campus. We had the university coaches and the Spanish language staff to teach us. We also had a lot of beer to drink in the evenings, which led to poor concentration in the endless Spanish labs the following day.

Instead of focusing on our primary sport, we were briefed on all sports. Most of us were not PE majors; we were just average athletes who did what we were told and, for the most part, didn't know why we did the training we were subjected to during our college years. It would have been a whole lot more beneficial to spend the majority of our time in the sport we would actually coach. A few of us were scrubbed for reasons no one could figure out but finally, we had a graduation ceremony and the survivors were given a week off before reporting to San Juan, Puerto Rico for the last leg of our training.

Puerto Rico was the first eye opener for most of us. After a night in a hotel, we met the next morning and were each given a slip of paper with the name of a slum in cities scattered around the island plus expense money and instructions to find a family to live with and a place to work in our sport for a one month period.

I was assigned to a famous slum in San Juan called La Perla, The Pearl. It is still there today and so are the signs warning visitors to enter at their own risk. La Perla was built on the beach, right below the walls of the famous Spanish fortress in Old San Juan, by poor people who scavenged the garbage thrown over the wall by the soldiers during the colonial period. In September of 1966, the shacks of the slum dwellers were mostly made of wood and set haphazardly in narrow alleyways.

Being totally naïve and with my swimming t-shirt on, a few words of Spanish in my vocabulary and a new crew cut to show off, I entered the slum. The first thing I noticed was the "Yanqui go home" graffiti on the walls. After several hours of discouraging results, I went back to the nearby YMCA where I'd left my suitcase and took a room for the night. The next day I found a swim club that agreed to allow me to be on deck with their coaches and then went back to La Perla to try my luck again. Finally, a guy at a tiny newspaper kiosk gave me directions to a house he said I could probably live in.

I found my way through the alleys and knocked on the door of a windowless shack. A woman came out and agreed to let me live in an attached room with her mother (she looked 80 and there was only one bed) for $7 a week, with meals. Being the ever clever guy I was, I asked her what would be the cost to share her bed. The answer was $8. As I was going through the process, a young boy came to the doorway, behind the woman and began to make signs with his thumbs and forefingers that looked like a large circle. I left the shack and went to the Y to get my bags, asking the boy if he could help. I was curious about the gesture he had made and he explained that he was indicating the size of her pussy, that she was a prostitute. Oh, well, the die was cast.

By the time we returned, it was dark and when we arrived at the door of my new home, we saw by candlelight a huge black guy shouting and waving a knife in my landlord's face. The boy yelled at me, "Run!" As we took off, he said, "Her husband." The neighbors had told him about the new renter and I guess he wasn't too happy with the idea.

So, after another night at the YMCA, I asked one of the staff for suggestions and he said he would accompany me to a shack where a PC volunteer had stayed the previous year. The middle-aged couple with two kids in their early teens was wonderful. They even gave me their bedroom which had a window and a breeze from the sea, cutting somewhat the stench of the garbage. The parents laid a mat for themselves on the kitchen floor. I gratefully stretched out on the bed in my underwear and fell asleep.

Sometime during the night, I had a nightmare that my body was covered with cockroaches. Slowly surfacing from the dream I realized that I was indeed covered by roaches, from head to toe. I breathed very shallow, weighing my limited options. Remembering the string attached to the bare light bulb overhead, on a count of three, I leaped up and pulled on it. With the light, the roaches scurried away. I sat up the rest of the night under that gleaming bulb.

When I was called to breakfast the next morning, I sat at the table and poured some milk into my bowl of cornflakes which forced the roaches in the bottom of the bowl to jump out. Making excuses about being late for a workout at the pool, I rushed off. The rest of the day I tried to come up with a plan for that night. The problem was that a PC rep would, sooner or later, be checking to see if I was actually staying in the slum.

That evening, I decided to have a drink (Cuba Libres were 25 cents) at a bar on the strip frequented by sailors from the nearby US Navy base, just blocks from La Perla. While I was sipping my first drink, the cute bar girl asked me if I was from one of the ships. I said, no, I lived in La Perla, and told her about my roach nightmare. Shocked that this all-American guy had to live in the slum, she invited me to spend the night with her. For the remainder of my stint in Puerto Rico, Maria and the other girls at the bar took me under their "wings" every night. The family in the slum was happy to get paid and covered for me with the PC. I received the education of a lifetime from those women, but not what you find advertised in Peace Corps brochures.

Soon, I was on my way to my assignment in Guayaquil, Ecuador, called La Perla del Pacifico, the Pearl of the Pacific. A large, ugly, sprawling city with miles of slums and unpaved roads that turned into quagmires during the rainy season, Guayaquil, when we lived there, was anything but a pearl. But in spite of the negatives, I loved it. It was a new world for me—a challenge, and an adventure. My first roommate and I spent more time than anyone in the small hotel we were assigned to until we finally found an apartment. We rented the second floor of a villa in a nice middle class neighborhood, just five blocks from the pool and track where we worked, and it wasn't long before our place was known as Grand Central Station. It was so nice that, often on weekends, volunteers from the agricultural projects who lived in the miserable slums would come in for R & R and crash at our place. We had a stereo, a great collection of albums, a fridge full of beer and a shoe box of good grass in the closet.

Soon, Ridge, my roomie, and I had another roommate, Gary Cleveland, a former US weightlifting champion who had placed fifth in the Tokyo Olympics. As the days went by, our apartment began to get pretty filthy. Early one morning, I heard a broom salesman peddling his wares in the street below and rushed out to buy us a broom. Having been told to bargain for everything, I was pleased when he accepted my counter offer of 26 *sucres* for the 30 *sucre* broom. Walking into the living room, I woke up Ridge to announce my purchase. When asked what I paid for it, he laughed, "You idiot, they go for seven *sucres* at the market." Another lesson learned.

Our local PC director brought me to the Piscina Olimpica, an aging 50-meter pool run by the municipality, to meet the people I would be working with. After a friendly reception, I invited the coaches to try a new plan, dividing the swimmers into specialty groups with one coach in charge of the sprinters, another, the distance group, another the breaststrokers, etc. Everyone seemed happy with the plan. The following day, I returned to the pool to find the coaches had all taken their original swimmers back. One of the coaches agreed to let me train his group and he would remain my assistant.

Remember that I had no previous coaching experience but I did have a huge advantage, I was American and people thought I knew more than I did. Coaching, to a great extent, is about getting across the idea to your athletes that you know exactly what you are doing. If the kids believe in you, they are capable of doing great things. And so it went.

When the first meet came, I looked at the schedule and told my group to be at the pool to warm up at 4 PM for the 5:30 starting time. At 4, we were the only ones at the pool. When we finished the warm-up, there still was no one there. At 5:15, a couple of people showed up. By 5:30, some other swimmers began to warm up. At 6, the ceremonies began, including a beauty contest with candidates from several provinces, folkloric dance performances and more than 30 minutes of speeches from various politicians and swimming officials.

One of my roommates showed up to watch the meet and, while waiting around for the endless activities to wind down, we commented rather loudly in the stands about how the fucking Ecuadorians couldn't get their shit together organizing the meet or anything else. After a while, I noticed a guy in the front row giving us the evil eye and I said to Steve that we better watch our language, somebody might understand English. The guy in the front row looked up at me and said, "Maybe better than you." It turned out he worked at the US Consulate and he tried unsuccessfully to get us kicked out of the country for slander.

The meet finally began at about 9 PM. By then, many of the swimmers were already sleeping in the stands. No further warm-up was allowed.

At the second meet, two months later, the tryouts for the South American Age Group Championships, my kids broke nine national records. I was chosen as one of the two coaches of the national team for the meet in Lima, Peru where two of my kids went on to win gold medals.

While at the meet in Lima, a rumor circulated that two of the Ecuadorian boys in the 13-14 age group had forged birth certificates and were actually 15 and 16 years old. I reported this to the head of the South American Swimming Confederation. The swimmers were eventually disqualified and their medals returned, and the President of the Ecuadorian Swimming Federation, Pepe Bejarano, was suspended.

Before Christmas, we were joined by our newest roommate, Steve Davis, a gymnastics and diving coach and a talented musician who later played for Commander Cody and his Lost Planet Airmen. Steve introduced us to the pleasures of smoking grass (and, yes, Bill Clinton, we did inhale). Steve played the guitar and sang and Gary played the harmonica. They seemed to know all the Dylan songs. I enjoyed just listening to the two of them, having been traumatized in the eighth grade by a music teacher who told me to just move my lips when singing. A couple of months later, Steve was busted by the Ecuadorian police trying to purchase some weed and was rushed out of the country with a deal that supposedly resulted in a gift of some jeeps to the local police.

Following Steve's departure, a meeting of all PC volunteers was held at the US Consulate where all volunteers who smoked grass were asked to stand up. It was quite ludicrous. No one did, of course, so we were all interviewed privately by the heads of our various groups. In my interview, I admitted having "tried it" but I said I didn't like it and hadn't smoked again. No one else was sent home.

In May 1967, at the tryouts for the Pan American Games to be held in Winnipeg that summer, two of my kids qualified, but a third was operated on for an emergency appendectomy only three days before the tryouts. The swimming federation agreed to give the boy a chance to make the team 10 days after the tryouts. Three days after the meet, with the doctor's permission and special stitches, he resumed training, swimming three times a day for one hour and building strength and endurance again the first week. At the time trial, Eduardo missed the qualifying time in the 400 freestyle by one second. With his two sisters, Tamara and Lolita, already qualified, his father decided to pay his son's expenses to the Games.

Meanwhile, though the Ecuadorian Swimming Federation decided not to send me, they were overruled by the Olympic Committee and I was chosen to be the national coach. But the Peace Corps denied me permission to go, first citing a PC rule that did not permit volunteers to set foot in the US during their term of service (they were afraid that we wouldn't want to go back to the host country after tasting the good life again). Since our flight was refueling in Miami and Minneapolis on the way to Winnipeg, technically, I would be violating PC policy. Next, the PC told me that an Ecuadorian coach should go so "they could learn from experience." I replied, in a letter to the head of the Peace Corps in Latin America, that if the Ecuadorians had been learning from experience for the last one hundred years, there would be no need for the PC. I decided to go anyway since the Ecuadorians were paying for the trip.

In those days, dating was not the norm among Ecuadorian women. Ecuador was a heavily Catholic country then. Virgin brides were still a big deal with the men. Often, young women didn't go out without a chaperone. It was common to see a guy holding hands with his girlfriend through the bars of the fence surrounding the girl's home. If you wanted to get laid, you went to a brothel or picked up a street walker, for as little as 25 cents. But occasionally, we got lucky. I once sat through the entire film, Dr. Zhivago, making out with a girlfriend. On another occasion, three of us gringos were walking down the street when we noticed a car slowly going by with three good looking young women in it. On the back window was a sticker from a US university. We yelled out to them to stop and they pulled over. After an introductory conversation, we were invited to the house of one of the women. When we got there, the door was opened by her mother who invited us in, sat us down, and asked if we were Catholics.

I replied, "No."

"Then, are you Protestants?" "No." "Evangelicals?" Again, "No." "Well, what religion are you?" "None." "Please leave my house immediately!" Oh, well...

I did meet a lovely young lady one day, the older sister of one of my swimmers. I was relegated to going to Berta's house and sitting on the living room couch next to her with the maid close by. When she repeatedly asked the maid to hand her water and cookies that were on the table right in front of her, I decided that it just wasn't meant to be and I never returned. Jumping ahead 30 years, Steve, Gary and I were back in Guayaquil in 1997 for a reunion. Many of my former swimmers showed up, and, unexpectedly, so did Berta, who still looked extremely good. She had just divorced, receiving a million dollar home in the settlement. My buddies and I were leaving for Quito, the capital city in the Andes, the next day and I asked her if she wanted to join us. She invited me over to her house and we discussed it further.

As soon as I got back to the hotel, I received a call from her: "I have to talk to you again," she said.

She drove over and, refusing to come up to my room, asked me to come down to the car where she said, "OK, you invited me, right?"

"Yes," I responded.

"Then that means you'll pay for everything, right?"

"Sure," I replied.

"OK, I'll meet you at the bus station in the morning."

So much for the million dollar house.

The next morning, at 6:30, the bus was pulling out about 15 minutes late when a car came screeching around the corner. Berta jumped out with her maid and two large suitcases (for the weekend). We yelled for the bus to stop, the maid put the luggage on the bus and Berta joined me in the next seat. We spent a pleasant day enjoying the spectacular scenery during the drive and train ride through the mountains. Finally arriving late at night at our hotel in Riobamba, high in the Andes, I went to the reception counter and asked for two double rooms.

Berta quickly told the guy, "No, a single and a triple."

Steve looked at me and said, "Powers, you waited 30 years and you are still not gonna get laid."

Sad but true. I went to Berta's room and asked what was going on. Her reply, "That is all you men ever want. What would people say? I have my place in society to think about."

I responded, "Berta, this may be your last chance to get laid and you blew it and, by the way, you are paying for your hotel room and you can get on the bus back to Guayaquil tomorrow."

I never saw her again.

One of my roomies found out that there was going to be a big party at a fancy house in the rich section of town and all the PC volunteers were invited. It turned out that the owner of the mansion was the Chief of Police of Guayaquil. His daughter had met one of the volunteers at a class in the university. For us, a party at a fancy house meant hard liquor which we couldn't afford on our $100 a month salaries. At one point, very drunk, I was taking a pee in the bathroom when I noticed that I was being watched by one of the numerous Christ figures in the house. This one was on the wall above the toilet. I went out and complained to Gary, too loudly, "You can't even take a piss here without Christ checking you out."

A guy in tuxedo, who looked like one of the waiters catering the party, stood nearby and heard my remark. Unfortunately, he was the Chief of Police. We were soon out on the street.

Someone came up with the bright idea to continue the party at my place and the girls agreed to join us, so, Gary and I rushed home, switched the living room bulb to a dark blue one, put on some tunes and brought out the beer. When the girls showed up, they sat around the edges of the room on chairs and refused to dance with anyone. It was time to shake them up a bit. Gary and I went around the corner and found a couple of prostitutes to come over. We walked in with the girls on our arms, went directly to one of bedrooms, leaving the door open and in loud voices proceeded to bargain for their wares. "What, 50 cents for a blowjob? That is an outrage! How much for straight sex?"

In no time, the society chicks had beaten a retreat back to their mansions. At least, we had a good laugh.

One night, Steve, Gary and I were having a few beers at a famous whorehouse called The Lay when a guy sitting across from us asked in broken English what we were doing in Guayaquil. We explained that we were with the Peace Corps. He asked how much we were paid and we told him, $100 a month.

"Can't live on that," he shouted, "Who is your boss?"

We told him it was this guy in Washington, Sargent Shriver, director of the Peace Corps. "Fuck Sargent Shriver," he yelled and proceeded to pay for our beers and offered to pay for the women, too. When we declined, he said "You come with me."

Where? "To the ship."

It turned out he was an engineer on a large banana boat—which was part cargo, part passenger—that plied the Pacific coast of the Americas. We jumped in a cab and rode the 20 miles to the port, arriving at about 2 AM. He got us through security and on to the boat where he took us to the crew's mess. We couldn't find a thing to eat so he said we should try the captain's kitchen. It was unlocked and we loaded up on trays of ham and cheese, bread and champagne. In his tiny cabin, we devoured as much as we could. While we were eating, he took out a stack of $100 dollar bills and threw them at us, then collapsed on his bunk. Our last instructions were, "What you don't eat, throw out the porthole" which we did to bury the evidence, just in case.

We left his money and quietly departed the boat just as the sun was coming up. The security guard saluted us as we left. Another night to remember in Guayaquil.

On another occasion, Ridge and I took our girlfriends to see a soccer game at the big stadium in town. When we got to the ticket counter, we were told the game had been sold out. Disappointed, we strolled back across the parking lot towards the Reyburger, the local version of McDonald's. Before we knew what hit us, we were surrounded by hundreds of very aggressive teenage beggars, demanding money. Ridge is 6' 5" and weighed over 200 pounds but we were trapped, and scared. Our plight attracted the attention of two policemen on horseback across the parking lot. They came at full speed swinging their batons and escorted us safely through the crowd.

Ridge and I went to a movie theater one afternoon. The balcony was for the poor people who paid about five cents for their tickets and sat on wooden benches. Below was the main floor where the fancier seats were. Often those sitting below were pissed on or hit by garbage thrown from the balcony. Ridge and I were watching the movie when something landed near us. We went up to the balcony to kick ass but when Ridge opened the curtain, we saw a guy robbing another at knifepoint. Running downstairs, we notified the manager and told him to call the police. The manager just laughed, "The police won't come. They are too scared to go into the balcony." Ridge and I went home.

Shortly after I arrived in Winnipeg for the Pan Ams, Gary called me from Washington. He, too, had been busted for buying grass and warned me that I would be kicked out as well, even though I was on the other side of the hemisphere at the time. Meanwhile, at the Games, one of the worst things I have ever seen happen to a swimmer happened to the boy who had gone to the meet with us after recovering from the appendix operation. By the time we arrived, he was back in good shape and we found that he was entered in the meet and in the heat sheets for his events.

His first event was the 400 IM. Eduardo was actually up on the blocks for his preliminary heat when, suddenly, the Ecuadorian representative ran over and pulled him down, disqualifying him from the meet. I leaped over the barrier and ran to the blocks calling the rep a lot of choice words, but to no avail. This was the same guy, Mr. Bejarano, who would soon be suspended for his involvement in forging the other swimmers' birth certificates. I was later told by another Ecuadorian official that he disqualified Eduardo to get revenge for my informing on him.

Soon after, I received a phone call from the Peace Corps in Washington asking me to go there after the Games to report on my experience. Knowing the real reason for the call and what my fate would be, I decided to take the Ecuadorian kids to Chicago for a week to show them the city, an opportunity they probably would never have again. Showing up in Washington a week late, I checked into the designated hotel and went to the PC office for my first meeting. Present were my country desk officer, Kirby Jones who became a long time advocate for better relations with Cuba, the director of PC Latin America, and the chief psychologist of the PC. The shrink gave me a piece of paper and pencil and told me to write down the names of all the volunteers who were smoking grass.

I don't know what he was thinking. I replied that I had no knowledge of anyone doing drugs. For three weeks, we went around in circles. Meanwhile, I was having a great time hitting all the clubs and concerts, getting exposed to some great music in this birth of the psychedelic era.

Finally, one day I was told that there would be a conference call with my country director in Ecuador, Eric Hoffmann, a former Nazi fighter pilot. If he agreed to have me back, I would be allowed to return. After about 30 minutes, the participants came out of the meeting and gave me a document to sign, telling me that the directorEric said he had signed statements from many volunteers saying I had been smoking grass.

If I signed the document resigning from the PC, nothing would go on my record. If not, they told me, I would have trouble ever finding a job again. Well, just 22 years old and still somewhat clueless, I denied any of the allegations but agreed to resign to avoid the threatened consequences. Three days later, I acquired a civilian passport and flew back to Ecuador. Going directly to the PC office in Guayaquil, I asked the city director about the signed statements. He replied that they had bluffed me out; they had absolutely nothing on me. They were afraid of the possible bad publicity if word got out that PC volunteers were "doing drugs." Welcome to the real world.

Two years later, on a visit back to Ecuador, the PC secretary told me the policy had changed and that volunteers were just told to be discreet about their use of marijuana.

Ironically, the PC was slow in canceling my payments at the local bank and I was able to receive my salary for three more months. I had returned to Ecuador to try and find a way to continue coaching my swimmers but their parents were too poor to pay me, so, I decided to pursue an offer in Caracas, Venezuela. On my way to the airport, a friend drove me first to the home of one of my swimmers for a final farewell. As I was getting out of the car, a drunk came up and asked for money. When I said no, he picked up a large chunk of concrete and was about to drop it on my head but my friend reached into the glove compartment and pulled out a gun. The drunk backed off and I made it to the airport intact. As the plane took off, I wept. Leaving those kids, my very first swim team, was more painful than leaving family.

When all is said and done, I still love Ecuador. Whenever someone asks me, "Where should I go in South America?" I always recommend Ecuador. A small country, situated in the northwestern part of the continent, just below Columbia, Ecuador has it all: beautiful Pacific coast beaches—many virtually untouched, the fabulous peaks of the Andes, the headwaters of the Amazon and that most amazing gem, the Galapagos Islands. All of these incredible spots are easy to reach and very inexpensive. For Americans, there is the added advantage that the US dollar is the local currency. On top of all this, they have the colorful indigenous tribes who produce the most exquisite handicrafts in all of South America.

Chapter II
Venezuela, 1967-1969

The year before, when I was in Peru for the age group meet, I met some Venezuelan swimmers and their parents and exchanged addresses. While in Ecuador I had received a job offer from the Italian-Venezuelan club and decided to take it. So, with my money running out, I bought a one way ticket to Caracas, leaving me with exactly $25 in my pocket. In Caracas, I was invited to stay in the apartment of one of the PC directors, Jim Stevens, who I had met at our training camp the previous year. Arriving on a late flight, I was not able to locate my host and had to stay at a cheap hotel for the night. With $15 left and getting a little nervous, I located Jim the next morning and moved to his penthouse apartment. Jim and I went to the job interview but as it turned out, the club was not looking for a coach, but a swim instructor for lessons. Since I had no desire to do that, I was back at square one.

The next day, I called up a Venezuelan family I had met at the swim meet in Peru and was invited for dinner. The following day, they invited me to see the pool at the Central University of Caracas where their kids trained. A day later, their coach resigned and I was immediately hired. For an atheist, I've always had someone watching over me. I stayed at UCV for the next two years and was appointed coach of Venezuela's national teams for both the South American and Central American Age Group Championships.

Throughout Latin America, one of the constants is the lack of professionalism in coaching. Unlike in the US where coaches share ideas and we all learn from each other's experiences, generally, south of the border, it is every coach for himself. After working for a year in Venezuela, I was told that there was going to be a coaches' meeting called by the chief Mafioso coach, Alfonso Victoria. I went with my friend, Jim Stevens. The coaches were to elect 12 members to the new coaches' association. There were 13 coaches present. I was coaching one of the top clubs in the country. After the vote, Jim asked Victoria why I had been left out. He replied that I had never bought him a beer—a slightly different criteria from what we would use in the US.

The US Ambassador to Venezuela at the time was a black guy who was holier than thou, constantly railing at the embassy staff to lead a moral life and not indulge in any activities that could reflect poorly on the US. There were a couple of bars that were loaded with prostitutes across the plaza from Jim's apartment. One evening, Jim walked in and spotted the Ambassador in a booth with a couple of prostitutes. He ran back home, got his camera and asked one of the other women in the bar to take a photo of the Ambassador with the prostitutes. When the photo appeared, mysteriously, on the Ambassador's desk, the morality campaign came to an abrupt end.

Though I didn't particularly like Caracas, its loud, oil rich and arrogant Venezuelans and their weird formalities (You couldn't enter a movie theatre without a sport jacket), I still managed to have fun. One time, leaving the pool during the Carnaval weekend, I ran into a group of about a dozen American hippies who were on spring break from a school in Barbados. They asked me if anything was going on so I recommended a trip on the cable car at night to the top of the mountain that overlooks Caracas on one side and the sea on the other.

I met them at their hotel and we crammed into a couple of taxis to go to the base of the mountain. After the ride up, we walked down a path a little ways and smoked a few joints to help us enjoy the view. As we were toking up at about dusk, one of the girls noticed several uniformed men heading down the path towards us. In near panic, we threw the remaining joints into a clump of weeds, only to be surprised as the uniformed men approached, that they were Cub Scouts. One of the girls had passed out in shock and we carried her back to the cable car entrance.

There was a long line waiting to go down but when the police saw us carrying the girl, I yelled, "She is sick, we need to get her to a doctor." They put us on the next car.

As I was saying goodbye to the hippies at their hotel, a car pulled up with another girl from their group who had gone dancing with two Chinese-Venezuelan guys she had met that day. I asked the two for a lift home and they said, "Hop in." At one point during the ride, I realized that I had switched to English and was so stoned that I couldn't seem to remember my Spanish. The car finally stopped and they told me to get out. I had no idea where I was and my watch showed it was almost midnight. I stood for what seemed like forever under a tree until I saw a man walking along the sidewalk. As he got closer, I realized he was my neighbor. He asked, "Rick, what are you doing out here?" I was standing in front of my own house.

Leaving another party in Caracas in the wee hours and no taxis anywhere, I tried to hitch a ride. Some lights were approaching and I put my thumb out. The van stopped and the two young guys in front said to jump in the back. I did, noticing that it was full of fresh bread and cakes. When I commented on how good it smelled, they said to just help myself. They had stolen the van minutes before. I got home safely and with several loaves of bread to boot.

Moving from country to country in Spanish-speaking Latin America could sometimes get you in trouble because what a word means in one country can be totally different in another. Early on, while coaching in Caracas, I was having a time trial at the pool. To even things up, I had my best male sprinter, Pedro, leave ten seconds behind the fastest girl. As I was ready to start the guy I yelled, "*Cogela!*" which means catch her, in Ecuadorian Spanish. But, in Venezuela it means "Fuck her." The parents in the stands were silent, in shock, but Pedro cracked up laughing and couldn't make it off the blocks.

Another time, in Brazil, my new assistant coach had just arrived from Argentina and one of the swimmers' families had invited us over for pizza. Oscar complemented the hostess on her great *pisa* which is pizza in Argentina but penis in Brazil. I cracked up at that one. The thumb and forefinger circled is A-Ok in the US but when I did it in Brazil to my swimmers in practice one day, they clued me in that it meant "Up your ass." Whoops!

Back in the late 60s, Venezuela had a small but vocal leftist movement. The university campus where I worked was considered autonomous, no police allowed. When the leftist guerrillas came to Caracas from the mountains, they could stay on campus, where they were usually safe from arrest. There was a branch of the Venezuelan Communist Party on campus, too. Being one of the few, if not the only American working on campus at that time, I was quite visible to the leftists. My board of directors of the swim club consisted of several graduate students, all of whom paraded their leftist credentials. I was hired by the university at the request of the parents of the swimmers but the student-controlled board often interfered and resented my presence. The worst incident that occurred was when the board failed to send in the team entries to a major meet. I was on the verge of resigning but the parents and swimmers pleaded with me to remain and were instrumental in forcing the resignation of the entire board.

One day, at the pool, I was on deck with my assistant coach when suddenly we heard automatic weapons fire coming from the parking lot on a rise beside the pool. We rushed up the hill and saw two guys, later identified as a leftist leader and a secret police agent dueling it out in the lot. We quickly ducked and yelled to the swimmers to run to the locker room. On another occasion, during practice, a group of students showed up on the grassy area next to the pool and began to make Molotov cocktails, running up the rise to throw them at the police on the highway below. When the army was called in to quell the demonstration, I actually got out with the students and threw a few rocks at the approaching soldiers, just to get a feel for the action. When the soldiers began to shoot the tear gas canisters, I got my ass out of there in a hurry.

One afternoon, before swimming practice, there was a Communist demonstration at the Economics building outside the pool complex protesting the use of an economics textbook perceived to be too capitalistic. I decided to give them a little competition and blasted some Beatles songs over the pool's loudspeaker system. The demonstrators complained to the athletic director about the loud music, and I was asked to turn it down. For the next several days, students showed up at practice time, jumping in the water in front of the swimmers, in spite of the very obvious signs prohibiting non-swim team members from using the pool from 3-6 PM.

One thing you learn early in the Latin culture is the macho mentality. Most guys will try to intimidate you with a lot of bluster. If you back down, you are dead meat. Nine times out of ten, they will back off if you are perceived to be unafraid. So, when the students jumped in, I went over and said, "Excuse me, but the pool is not open to the public during swimming practice."

Their rote response was, "I am a university student. I will swim whenever I want to."

Which triggered my response, "Get out of the pool, asshole, before I drag you out."

Invariably, they got out.

A couple of quiet days went by, then, one afternoon, I heard a lot of shouting in the distance that was getting closer by the minute. Before I knew what was happening, hundreds of students had poured into the grandstand around the pool, locked the pool doors and shouted at the swimmers to leave. I was surrounded and forced to go up into the stands to be put on trial. The guy in charge was the head of the local branch of the Communist Party. He introduced himself to me and declared that I was charged with insulting many students and would be tried and, if found guilty, I would no longer be allowed to work there.

"Who has a complaint against the American?" he asked the mass of students.

One stood up and said, "He called me an asshole."

I was given my opportunity and I responded, "First, you don't know how to read, because the signs clearly say the pool is closed to the public at the time you came in. Second, I asked you in a nice way to leave. When you answered rudely, yes, I told you to get your ass out of the pool."

When asked to respond, the student remained silent. The "judge" then asked if there were other complainants. When no one said anything, he shocked the hell out of me when he told the crowd, "Students, you must treat him like a university professor, with respect."

He also told me to notify him if there were any more problems. That night I slept soundly.

The next afternoon, as I was putting on my swimsuit in the locker room, I noticed a teenager who, on a previous occasion, had been caught stealing wallets from the lockers. I called the guard to eject him. When I went up on deck to coach the 10 and under age-group kids, the same guy was in the stands right by the pool, and he started swearing at me. I told him not to use that language in front of the little kids but he did it again. I asked him if he wanted to step outside and take care of the problem but again he swore at me, at which point I jumped up in the stands and shoved him. The second I made contact, I was surrounded by five guys who had been hiding behind a large tree at the edge of the pool, one of whom shoved a pistol into my stomach shouting "Now he's hitting university students."

It all happened so fast. What saved me were the 30 little kids who pushed in to see what was happening to their coach. Someone called the athletic office and a group of coaches came running to my aid wielding baseball bats. The gunman and his cronies ran off.

I was told by the rector of the university never to confront those guys again. Several of my friends offered me guns over the next few days which I did not accept. I could just see myself walking the pool deck with a stop watch in one hand and a pistol in the other. I've always wondered if that would make the swimmers train harder. Returning from a meet in Puerto Rico two weeks later, I was told that the guy with the gun had been jailed for murder. Meanwhile, the university was closed again by the army due to more demonstrations. Prudence dictated that it was time to move on.

San Tome was an oil camp, a subsidiary of Gulf Oil, in southern Venezuela. It was a compound of some 200 American families living in the middle of nowhere. They had a swim team, though, and the previous year, they had invited me to bring the national team to train for a week at the camp, in exchange for some help for their young swimmers. When I left Caracas, I was communicating with a Brazilian who had offered to find me a coaching job in Brazil, out of gratitude for my help in recommending a swimming scholarship for his son in the US. I decided to take an offer from San Tome until the Brazil job came through. So for the next six months, I lived in the camp in utter boredom.

I was just about the only single person there and one of the few who didn't speak English with a southern accent. The main activity on the camp was downing shots of bourbon at the club bar while the Texans and Oklahomans argued about whose college football team would win that year. In addition to the bar, there was a four lane bowling alley where I killed some time. I threw a couple of parties at my house but the Venezuelan workers who lived in the compound across the highway would crash the parties and steal my cologne, booze and record albums. So, I stopped that.

I did meet a guy from San Francisco who worked for another company that serviced the drilling equipment. He had an encyclopedia of natural drugs and the plants and the countries where they could be found. There was one drug listed that was supposedly found only in a grove of trees in Southern Venezuela, in a semi-desert region not far from where we lived.

We borrowed a pickup one day and drove out to find the place. Locating the village which was supposed to be close to the trees we were looking for, we began questioning the local people. Most of the villagers just ignored us but one old man asked why we were looking for that tree. Our cover story was that my friend's sister had a serious illness and we heard about the medicinal properties of the drug from the tree and hoped to bring some back to cure her. He took us to his shack which was just a thatched roof over four tree trunks and open to the wind. He asked if we would like to try the drug, and we said, "Sure."

He pulled out a pocket knife and scraped some powder off one of the trunks holding up his house. "Snort it up," he said, and we did. There was an instant head rush. Then he picked up an axe and we drove to a grove of trees. Chopping off a large branch, he threw it in the pickup and off we went. The old guy had told us that you could make tea from the bark and dry the wood to get the powder.

Fast forward another eight years. In 1977, I left Brazil and took another job in Venezuela. John, the San Francisco guy, and I stayed in touch over the years and, coincidently, he moved to Brazil the same week I returned to Venezuela. We gave each other contacts where we could purchase weed. When I called his contact in Caracas, his mom answered and I asked for her son, saying I was a friend of John's. She told me that her son had just been transferred to Trinidad but she insisted I come over for dinner. She was the perfect Yiddish mama and she prepared a feast for me. When I finally got up to leave, she asked me to wait just one minute and went somewhere in the back of the house. Returning with a brown paper bag, she said, "I believe this is what you came for."

I looked inside and, yes, it was filled with marijuana! In a very matter of fact tone, she said, "I just don't want my son to have trouble with the police, so I grow it in my garden."

By January, 1970, the Brazil job was confirmed and I made my next move to the only Portuguese-speaking country in South America.

Chapter III
Porto Alegre, Brazil, 1970-72

Brazil, which is larger than the continental United States, is a vast and diverse country rich in natural resources. But like all of Latin America, it has a history of corrupt, inept governments whose policies have hampered economic progress and led to social inequities. The *favelas* (slums) of Rio de Janeiro are known throughout the world. Similar slums ring all Brazilian cities. An estimated 15 million homeless children roam the streets. Street violence makes living in the cities a challenge. Everyone I know in Brazil, myself included, has been robbed or assaulted at least once.

The Brazilian people as a whole are warm and generous, fun to be with. The food is incredible with a variety of fruits that is almost unreal, and a range of options that will satisfy any palate. The music is fantastic, the women exquisite, and, don't even mention the endless beaches, the best in the world. From the mysteries of the Amazon, the spectacular Iguacu waterfalls to the Lencois de Maranhao (a stretch of pure white sand dunes and rain water lagoons in the northern state of Maranhao) and the wonderful colonial areas of Ouro Preto, Parati, Olinda and Salvador, Brazil has amazing sites waiting for the adventurous tourist. The beauty of Rio de Janeiro is unmatched by any major city in the world.

Leaving Venezuela, I took a quick vacation in Ecuador to visit my former swimmers and waited there for my new employer to mail me my ticket to Brazil. When the ticket arrived, I found that it was booked as Brazil-Ecuador instead of Ecuador-Brazil. The airline wouldn't honor it.

29

So, I was forced to buy another ticket, which just about finished off my remaining funds. I am amazed today how I lived from day to day, even without health insurance, back then. The ticket I bought read Guayaquil-Sao Paulo-Porto Alegre. When I arrived in Sao Paulo, my bags were not on the plane. By the time I had filled out the requisite forms regarding my missing baggage, my connecting flight had departed. I had no choice but to spend the night in a hotel. Thinking I was in Sao Paulo, I took a taxi and told the driver, in Spanish, to take me to a hotel in the center of Sao Paulo, where I was told I could pick up my bags the next morning.

The only problem was that Sao Paulo was 100 kilometers away. The international airport at the time was in Campinas, another city, but that was not what was written on the ticket. So, after the rip-off taxi ride and the hotel cost, I went to the airline office the next morning to get my bags, which had arrived. But now, it turned out that I had missed the daily flight to Porto Alegre again. The person at the airline recommended I take a bus to Porto Alegre, which was all I could afford with my diminished funds. So I did. Well, 21 hours and two hot dogs later, the bus arrived in Porto Alegre. I took a cab to the swimming club with my last remaining dollars and spent an hour at the entrance gate. The idiot guard wouldn't let me in because I didn't have a club membership card and he didn't understand my Spanish or English. Finally, a club member helped me out and I got a much-needed shower.

Gremio Nautico Uniao, the premier sports and social club in Porto Alegre, Brazil's largest southern city, became my home for the next two years.

In Porto Alegre, a city where thousands of Italians and Germans had settled and blondes were almost as common as in Europe, I upped the ante in terms of the professional challenge. Brazil had long dominated swimming in South America. Gremio Nautico Uniao had a tradition of finishing in the top 10 at Nationals. We had great facilities, a 50-meter outdoor pool, 25-meter indoor, diving and teaching pools. And I had several assistants. We were really the only game in town, in fact, in the state. So, in order to find challenging competition, we had to travel quite far.

Living in Brazil meant that I had to learn about the Brazilian passion, soccer. Not long after I arrived, the 1970 World Cup preliminary games began in Mexico City. Brazil still counted on the legendary Pele in those days. The day before the first game, my swimmers asked if we could train early the next day so they could go home and watch the game on TV. Of course, I said no, reminding them that they were swimmers, not soccer players. Well, when our practice ended the next day, the swimmers rushed off with their clothes under their arms. I had no idea what was going on and, after showering, leisurely left the club to go home. As I walked out the gate, the first thing that struck me was that there was not a single car on the busy street fronting the club. As I strolled down the street, suddenly, from every window, I heard people shouting, "GOAL!" Someone saw me on the sidewalk and invited me into their home to watch the rest of the game.

I caught the fever. Brazil won the Cup for the third time and the country went wild. People painted their cars half green, half yellow. A school holiday was declared. It was a great introduction into the culture of the country that dominates South America in so many ways. While I was there, my swimmers took me to a couple of games.

The fans can be a bit unruly. Everyone is patted down for weapons upon entering the stadium. The fans of the two local professional teams wear either red or blue shirts to the games and sit on opposite sides of the stadium. One half is a sea of red, the other blue. Since they cannot bring weapons, they bring plastic bags, piss in them and hurl the piss bombs at the opposing team's fans. It's kind of hard to focus on the game while ducking piss bags.

The second time I went, my girlfriend came along. She was wearing very tight jeans. As we came into the stadium from the ramp, virtually every fan on our side of the stadium stood up and chanted "*Bunda, Bunda*," which translates into "nice ass." Needless to say, very few women attended the games.

Shortly after, that girlfriend announced to me that she was pregnant. I asked her what had happened to her birth control pills. She had decided that having a baby would be a way to get out of her parents' house and stop being subject to the abusive relationship she had with her father. It took about a week to convince her to have an abortion. Abortions were illegal then in Brazil. I checked with the club doctor and he made an appointment with a well-known doctor. It was an interesting experience. We walked in to the waiting room in a fancy office in a well known location. There were some eight to ten obviously wealthy women sitting around waiting for their turn and chatting about how they got knocked up. I was the only guy there. After the procedure, I took my friend home and we both went our separate ways. Soon, I moved to Sao Paulo. Thirty five years later I ran into her again in Porto Alegre. After chatting for a while, it became apparent that she had no recollection whatsoever of having gotten pregnant and having the abortion.

That year, 1971, we finished in fourth place at the National Championships with a South American record and three national records. I was psyched up for the coming year.

Another brief digression: after leaving the Peace Corps and moving to Venezuela, I received a notice to report for my army physical in Chicago (a.k.a. the Peace Corps' revenge). Citing lack of funds, I requested that I be allowed to take the exam at a US base in Panama. Permission was granted and I went to Panama on the second day of the Carnaval celebration in 1968. I found a bed for $2 in the dorm at the local YMCA and asked the black locker room attendant if there was anything fun going on that night related to Carnaval. He told me to meet him at 10 pm, after he got out of work. We got on a bus and drove for almost an hour. When we got off, we headed across the street to a large barn-like structure. Entering, I was a bit apprehensive to see that I was, apparently, the only white person in a crowd of hundreds of blacks who were singing, dancing and drinking like it was going out of style. My friend introduced me around and that broke the ice. We partied till dawn.

The next morning, I took my physical which I passed, and went back to Caracas. A couple of weeks later, I was called for induction into the army in Chicago. Pleading lack of funds again, I didn't go. I then heard that my local draft board was fire bombed, and for the next two years, I went under the government's radar.

In 1970, now in Brazil, I was told by my parents that another letter had arrived telling me to present myself for induction. At the time, I was months away from my 26th birthday which would have put me over the draft age limit. I asked one of the doctors at the club to write a letter to my draft board telling them I had a severe form of hepatitis and could not travel. In addition, the US consul in Porto Alegre, Robert Gelbard, a close friend, wrote a letter confirming my illness. After my birthday in September, I again wrote the draft board notifying them that I was now healthy, thinking that they could no longer pester me. But unknown to me, the draft law had been changed and the age limit was now 35.

The draft board never answered my letters so, I let another six months go by then decided to visit my parents in Chicago. The plane was to stop off in New York City where I would spend a couple of days with one of the stewardesses on my flight who I was dating. As we went through customs, everyone received a gray card to fill out. I was given a red one and told to wait on one side. In walked two stereotypical looking FBI agents in long white raincoats who asked if I was Rick Powers and told me I was under arrest for failure to heed the draft notice.

One of the agents asked what I did and I told him I coached swimming. He said he had three kids on a swim team and that they wouldn't worry about handcuffing me. I was booked and allowed to call my cousin who promised to come right over to post bail. Somehow, Roy got lost in the city he had spent his whole life in and showed up at one minute to five, as I was being led out of the lockup to the vans to be transported to the real prison. The guy behind the desk yelled, "Is there a Rick Powers here?"

I said, "That's me," and he replied, "You are lucky," as he took off the cuffs.

I was sent to Chicago for the trial.

When I arrived in Chicago, my father, a long time labor union organizer, asked around and came up with a good lawyer who often defended draft resisters. We went to court and were dismayed to find out that my trial judge was Julius Hoffman of The Chicago Seven Trial fame. He had a reputation as a hanging judge who always sided with the government. We began to look at other options. One day, while passing a local recruiting station, I decided to find out what the difference was between being drafted and enlisting. I walked in and was soon seated in front of the bemedalled sergeant in charge. His first question was, "Have you ever worked for the US Government?"

When I said that I had been in the Peace Corps, he immediately closed his book and said, "We consider the Peace Corps to be a subversive organization. We don't want you."

So, I could be drafted, but I could not enlist. It was not ours to reason why…

Later that day, my Dad and I went to the local Quaker office and set up a trip on the Underground Railroad to Canada, just in case nothing else worked. Our home phone was being tapped so we made all calls from public pay phones. In the end, what we worked out, through the lawyer, my Dad's union contacts and our Congressman, Abner Mikva, the first member of the House to publicly oppose the war, was a deal whereby the government would drop the charges if I would agree to be inducted.

I went for my physical after popping a couple of amphetamines. At one point, a black kid about 18 and I were seated in a room answering the written test, which was one part vocabulary, one part identifying designs of various types of machines. The officer sat us down on opposite sides of the classroom and told us to knock on the door across the hall when we were finished. I had no idea what any of the machines were and wondered what I was going to answer when the black kid asked if I could help him with the vocabulary questions. I said, sure, but can you help me with the machines? So we helped each other. After turning in our test sheets, we waited about five minutes. Suddenly, the door flew open and the officer stormed in, grabbed the black kid by the collar, and dragged him down the hall yelling, "I know you cheated!" In a city where just a few years before, all the beaches and most neighborhoods were segregated, that incident wasn't entirely out of character.

Next, I was in a group getting our blood pressure taken. The doctor pulled me aside and asked if I wanted to enter the army. I didn't know what to reply. Was it a trick question? But he said, "Look, I am against this war. Your blood pressure is high but we know people are taking drugs to raise it so you have to be checked again tomorrow." When I said, "No, I don't want to go in," he told me to stay up all night, get drunk and find

Dr. Joe the next morning and tell him that he sent me. The next morning, Dr. Joe raised my blood pressure even higher and gave me a deferment.

We went back to court and the prosecutor had to drop the charges because I had complied with my part of the deal "in good faith." During the time I was awaiting trial, the government denied ever receiving any of the letters I had sent to my draft board the previous year. As I was leaving the courtroom after the charges were dismissed, the government prosecutor walked up to my lawyer and said, with a smirk on his face that I'll never forget, "Oh, by the way, those letters your client alleged to have sent to the draft board, we just found them. It seems they got filed in the wrong drawer." Twenty four hours later, I was on a plane back to Brazil.

Swim meets in South America are always a challenge, not so much in terms of the normal stress which every coach is subject to, but because of the unexpected things that often ruin the experience. In Porto Alegre, we had a president of the state swimming federation who I was always at odds with. On one occasion, Mr. Risco walked into the indoor pool area where we had our winter meets and lit a cigarette in front of the "No Smoking" sign. I had the swimmers chant "No Smoking" but, in his arrogance, he wouldn't put out his cigarette. When the meet started, in the 100 free, I had the swimmers dive and each swim different strokes, which is all legal under the term "freestyle." He disqualified all of them.

At another meet, as I was cheering on my swimmers, Mr. Risco announced, "No cheering is permitted by the coaches." I flipped him off from the other side of the pool. On the way to a meet in Sao Paulo, he ordered the boys and girls to sit on opposite sides of the bus. One of our oldest swimmers, the team leader, stood up and ripped a fart right in his face. At night, in the hotel, another swimmer slid an ampoule smelling of rotten eggs under his door. While the whole team waited expectantly behind closed doors, he staggered out into the hall choking and screaming that he would get us for it. Soon, he was suspended by the national federation for investing $10,000 sent to him to purchase an automatic timing system in his own personal business.

On another occasion, I arranged a club trip to Montevideo, Uruguay for a meet. We were housed in the dorm rooms at the host club. The night the meet finished, I went with a group of the older boys to cruise the waterfront nightlife. When we arrived back at the swimming club at dawn, frantic parents were waiting at the door. We were unaware that that same night the Tupamaro guerillas had kidnapped a CIA agent in Montevideo and the government had declared a curfew. We could have been shot on sight for being out on the streets.

In the summer of 1971, the Pan Am Games were held in Cali, Columbia. Since I had the only distance swimmer on the Brazilian team, I was told by the Brazilian official in charge that I could go to the national training camp in Rio before the games and continue to prepare him. When I arrived, the national team coach, Roberto Pavel, told me not to enter the pool. I asked him if we could, at least, discuss Gustavo's training so he would be aware of where he was in terms of his conditioning. Pavel replied that no, he would take over and it was not my problem anymore.

I actually went to watch the games and trained one of my former Ecuadorian swimmers while I was there. Meanwhile Gustavo was forced to train with the sprinters and proceeded to have a lousy meet. After the games, Coach Pavel wrote in his report to the Brazilian sports federation that Gustavo's poor performance was due to the fact that I had refused to give him advice on Gustavo's workouts. Gustavo, an extremely hard worker, was disappointed, to say the least, and decided to quit swimming.

In Cali, I was hanging around with a guy from the US gymnastic team. One night he decided to steal the Cuban flag in the plaza at the Pan Am Games village. The Cubans, though, ever vigilant, caught him and gave him quite a beating. It was a common sight at the village, in the evenings, to see many athletes laying around, resting on the grass. What was really going on was that Columbian drug dealers were exchanging marijuana for the team uniforms of the athletes who were simply stoned.

I also lost my top female swimmer that summer. At the trials for the Pan Am games, she was warned by her jealous boyfriend, another of my swimmers, not to swim hard at the trials because he didn't want her to be away for long. When she complied with his request, I suspended her from the team. She later married the guy and was physically abused for years until she eventually found the courage to leave him.

The second year in Porto Alegre, having lost my two national champions, I had a much younger, less experienced team to prepare. At a regional one day meet, I entered two of my girls in only one event each in order to focus on qualifying for the upcoming nationals. Both qualified but as we were celebrating, the swimming director of my club came over and fired me. His reasoning was that by having the girls swim only one event each, the club had lost points. I went home in shock, but 30 minutes later, one of the parents showed up and said, "Come back to the club with me and let's talk to the director."

I said, "No way, the guy is a nutcase."

After he convinced me that it would be ok, we went back, sat down with the director and had a Coke. He had apparently forgotten that he had fired me and everything was fine again. Crazy stuff.

When nationals rolled around, I went first to the age group nationals and then planned to go back to Porto Alegre for the final week of the senior swimmers taper. I received a call from the swimming director saying I was prohibited from returning to Porto Alegre but should meet the swimmers at the competition venue the following week. The bottom line was, I didn't see my senior swimmers for the crucial part of their taper. After the nationals, where we finished in fifth place, I returned home with the swimmers to be told by my nemesis, the swimming director, that I could continue coaching if I agreed to a 50 percent salary cut. Several other coaches of different sports were fired on the excuse that the club was cutting back on sports expenses in order to build a dance hall. 35 years later the dance hall still hasn't been built.

The large Brazilian clubs had a board of directors that set club policy and priorities. As rival candidates jockeyed for power, a new board could reverse previous policy and decide to make budget cuts in any area, even eliminating a sport entirely. This often happens in Brazil and it doesn't give coaches much job security. I resigned from my position at Gremio Nautico Uniao in February 1972.

One of the best assistant coaches I ever had was Mauri Fonseca, my assistant at GNU, who later became a national coach himself. He is an extremely generous person who has been a lifelong friend. Another of my assistant coaches, Camelo and I were having dinner one evening at a well-known restaurant when a blackout occurred. In the pitch black dining area, we began making barking and purring noises. Soon we were joined by the other patrons in a din of howls, roars, moos, etc. When suddenly, the lights came back on and we looked around, to our astonishment, all the other diners were elderly people with serious looks on their faces. Camelo and I couldn't eat from laughing so hard.

I had a favorite family in Porto Alegre—the Beckers. Three of their girls were on the swim team. They were of German heritage and spoke perfect English, too. Theirs was one of those homes where you walked in the door, kicked off your shoes, and felt truly "at home." Over the years, the mom always asks me when I visit, "Did you get married yet?" When I reply, not yet, she says "Who is going to care for you when you get old?"

A couple of years ago when she asked me the same question again, one of the daughters said, "Mom, don't worry, he has ten women in this city who will take care of him." A slight exaggeration but it is truly a place where I could live and feel comfortable.

Mariana, one of the daughters, is a well known TV sports announcer in Rio. One year, giving a clinic for the Federal University of Rio, I discussed relaxation exercises and visualization for the swimmers. I cited an experience I had with Mariana in Porto Alegre when I was staying at her family's home. I pointed out that in addition to the mental preparation, the exercises also help you relax and induce sleep if you do them in bed. And I told them about one night when I slept in Mariana's room, but in another bed....

Suddenly all the students in the audience drowned me out, shouting, "Oh, sure!"

I said, "No, really."

Again, they shouted "Oh, sure!"

I don't think they ever believed me but I went on with the story. Mariana had been stressed out and not sleeping well for some time so I said I would show her some exercises to help her reduce the stress and fall asleep. I began guiding her through the isometric contractions and subsequent relaxation when, the next thing I knew, I was waking up. It was morning. And when I looked around, the other bed was empty. I went down the hallway opening doors to find her. When I opened the maid's door, there she was in the maid's bed.

"What are you doing here, Mariana?"

"Well, you started those damned exercises and in no time you were snoring so I had to find another place to sleep."

Well, they worked for me, at least.

Chapter IV
Sao Paulo, Brazil, 1970-77

I went job hunting for the next two months, visiting several clubs in Brazil, even traveling to Chile, and visiting the Cuban embassy to see if there were possibilities in Cuba. This was barely a year before the US-sponsored coup overthrew President Allende in Chile.

One of the people I contacted was the same man who had helped me get the job at Gremio Nautico Uniao. This extremely wealthy *carioca* (a person from Rio de Janeiro) called a friend of his in Sao Paulo who was one of the directors of the Jewish Community Center there, called A Hebraica de Sao Paulo. I went for an interview where I was jokingly told I would have to be circumcised to work there. Responding that I already was, I am convinced, clinched the job.

My new club was quite an incredible place. With about 20,000 members, four swimming pools, including an almost completed 50-meter pool, a library, theatre, basketball gymnasium that could seat 6,000, twenty tennis courts, numerous restaurants, etc, it was like a small city. What it didn't have was much of a swim team. But, building from the ground up isn't really so bad, sometimes.

The swimmers we had were young and enthusiastic, easy to mold, easy to break bad habits and, in the Jewish community, were under a lot of pressure to succeed, which has its positives and negatives. Doing well in school and the business world is not the same as doing well in sports, though.

My first abbreviated season we did not have a single national qualifier, so, our taper was going to be for the state meet in the nearby city of Mogi das Cruzes.

Ever since the 1968 Olympics, I had wanted to try a full rest taper that had been used by the Aussie swimmer, Michael Wenden to defeat Don Schollander, the American hands-down favorite in the 100 and 200 free events. Since, during the intervening years, I was always coaching some pretty good teams and they continued to swim well utilizing the traditional taper, which still included long rest, all out sprints (timed 50s and 25s right up to the last couple of days before the big meet), I was afraid to risk something radically different. Now I had the perfect situation, a group of relatively new swimmers who had nothing to lose. As it turned out, we had a very good meet with significant time drops. The following year, two of the boys won medals at nationals.

After my tenure in Porto Alegre, I had built a reputation in Brazil. I had been clear, when hired by the Jewish Community Center, that the club must open its doors to non-Jewish swimmers. What many of the top clubs in Brazil did was give scholarships to athletes to train and represent the club but without the rights of the paying members to use other club facilities. To my dismay, no one wanted to transfer to the JCC. Anti-semitism was alive and well in Brazil. When my best swimmer, of German heritage, from Porto Alegre moved to Sao Paulo I was sure she would join my club. Her father was apologetic but said his daughter would never represent a Jewish club.

Across the street from our club was the Pinheiros (Pines) Club, which was twice our size and one of the top clubs in Brazil. It had been primarily a German club and during World War II, relations between the clubs were strained, to say the least. Shortly after my arrival, I walked over to introduce myself to the Pinheiros coach. He proceeded to lecture me on why Brazilians would never be any good at swimming. He was using the Olympic swimmer workouts from Doc Counsilman's book, "The Science of Swimming" to train his age group kids.

Finally, after a year, a Pinheiros swimmer showed up at my club. He had just had a fight with his coach and wanted to know if he would be welcome. With his arrival, everything changed. We ended up with a couple dozen scholarship swimmers, not only from Sao Paulo clubs but from as far away as Porto Alegre and even Argentina. It was a great experience for all the kids. They broke down old prejudices and formed friendships that, more than 30 years later, are still warm. We even had a family of 3rd generation Syrians, the Latufs, though their acceptance into the club took a special decision by the board.

We had met the Latuf kids at local swim meets but they lived in another city, Ribeirao Preto, around a three-hour drive from Sao Paulo. One Saturday afternoon, I and three of my older swimmers drove out to attend the wedding of my assistant coach. He was a nice guy, but a bit slow. He lived in a small town, which is not on any map, but within the state of Sao Paulo. We got lost and finally stopped to ask directions at a pharmacy in another town. The pharmacist asked why we wanted to go there. We replied, "A wedding."

"Who is getting married?"

When I mentioned the guy's name, he said, "Who would want to marry him?"

He did give good directions, though, and we arrived at the church just as the ceremony was ending. The bride was quite good looking. We all headed to a large barn-like building down the block in the one-street town for the reception and party. I was told that I was the first American to visit the town and the local kids came up to touch me.

My swimmers and I were seated at a small wooden table and were served skewers of meat from the cow that had been killed for the wedding. In addition, though all the other guests were served glasses of beer, ours came in pitchers. I wasn't too drunk to dance so, when the music began, I asked a nice-looking woman if she would like to dance. As we slow-danced my hand went down to caress her butt.

The groom was suddenly in my face. "Run to the car, her husband is coming with a gun!"

The four of us made record time to the car but we were too drunk to drive all the way to Sao Paulo. I remembered the Syrian family in Ribeirao, not far from where we were. We drove in on a Saturday night when young people in the smaller towns cruise back and forth on the main street. I asked a couple of teenagers if they knew where the Latuf family lived and, of course, they did. We found their home and the father let us sleep on newspapers on the floor of the new house he was building next door.

The next day, Sunday, he invited us to stay for a BBQ at the country club they frequented and over a few more beers I invited his four kids to join our club. They were all national level swimmers and a lot of fun, too. They recruited three more local swimmers for my team, as well.

I would go out to Ribeirao every few weeks for the weekend to check on how they were doing and they would spend vacations training with us in Sao Paulo. Their mom was an excellent cook who made the most wonderful fresh yoghurt and all the famous Middle Eastern dishes. What a treat it was to visit them. One of the boys, Marcio, is today a Brazilian national team coach.

While in Porto Alegre I had attempted to apply for a work permit but my application vanished at the Justice Ministry. So I was forced to leave the country every six months to renew my tourist visa. In Sao Paulo, the club insisted that I try again. First, I turned in my police clearance from Chicago; next, I took the physical exam which involved stool, urine and blood tests. Returning to pick up the results two days later, the woman at the counter shook her head and said, "You have syphilis. Get cured and come back after."

I said there was no way that I had syphilis, and asked her to please do another test. She refused. I went to the club doctor and he sent me to a lab for another blood test. It came out negative and I took the result back to the government lab where the woman there refused to even look at it. Next, my doctor had me undergo another blood test at the University of Sao Paulo lab, considered the best in South America. Again, the result was negative and again, it was rejected by the government lab. After I was told that they didn't accept tests from anyone else, my doctor advised me to wait two months and then return and tell them that I had been treated. And so I was retested and the result was negative. The same woman told me that if I had followed her instructions and gotten cured immediately, it wouldn't have taken so long.

At this point, I was told to take the exam results to an office in Rio de Janeiro, a six-hour bus ride. When I handed over the results to the inspector there, he just shook his head. "Blood test is fine but the feces and urine have expired. Return to Sao Paulo and do them over again."

A couple of weeks later, I returned to Rio and was told that everything was in order and the application would be sent to the Justice Ministry in Brasilia, the capital. Three months went by, then six and still no word. Eventually, the club sent someone to Brasilia to find out where my visa was. He discovered that the one person in Brazil who could stamp the visas for foreigners was on a one-year sabbatical in Europe.

Finally, almost four years since I had originally applied in Porto Alegre, I received my visa. Patience is not only a virtue but a necessity in the third world. Three years later when I was returning to Venezuela, I thought I would preempt these problems by applying for a Venezuelan work visa before I left Brazil. I received the visa, took the flight to Venezuela, got off the plane in Caracas to drop off my bags and tried to continue on for a vacation in the US. I was denied permission to board the plane because, since I had a work visa, I had to have proof before I boarded that I had paid taxes on my earnings. I showed the person that I just got off the plane an hour ago and hadn't started work yet but he was adamant and told me that I had to go to the Immigration Department and get the tax document.

It was Friday afternoon, my luggage was already on the plane and now I was stuck with the clothes on my back until I could get to the immigration office on Monday morning. I stayed the weekend with friends. Bright and early on Monday I was at the office. The person in charge said "How can you have the tax paper if you haven't worked yet?"

"My contention exactly," I replied. But he said to wait while he consulted with his boss.

When he came back he said they had decided to charge me 40 percent of the value of my airfare from Brazil to Venezuela in lieu of paying taxes. They just made it up on the spur of the moment. In the end, the club reimbursed me and I did make a late Monday flight to the US.

Even though my team began from a very basic level, I always felt that meets, in addition to the few scheduled by the swimming federation, were a learning experience necessary for motivation, as well as a fun experience for the swimmers. My first year at the Hebraica club, I organized several dual meets, in addition to the regularly scheduled regional meets. We got our butts kicked but we steadily improved. As the swimmers got faster, other teams didn't want to score points anymore, and by the fourth year only two teams in the country would compete with us at all. In many countries it is all about losing face.

In 1975, I took the team to the US, finishing the trip in St. Louis, hosted by my childhood coach's team, the Jewish Community Center of St. Louis. I was so proud to show him what I had accomplished.

In 1973, I was selected to coach the team that represented Brazil in the Maccabiah Games in Israel. It was my first trip out of the Americas. We had a wonderful experience and following the meet traveled for several days in Israel. One day, two of the swimmers and I hired a taxi to take us to Masada, the mountain top fortress near the Dead Sea, where a group of Jewish fighters once held off a Roman army for years, the survivors eventually committing suicide when their water ran out. We were told to climb the mountain early in the morning, to avoid the oppressive desert heat that would come later. Of course no one wanted to wake up early so we ended up arriving at the base of Masada at about 10 AM.

Beginning the climb without water and wearing just shorts and t-shirts, we were soon regretting sleeping in that morning. There was not another soul going up at that time of day, just us idiots. Finally, totally exhausted and dehydrated, we arrived at the entrance to the fortress only to discover two things: One, there was an entrance fee, and two, we had left our money in the taxi. As we were standing there pondering our next move, a large group of tourists began to leave, heading for the cable car to descend. I told the swimmers to wait a minute and plunged into the group. Lo and behold, they were speaking Portuguese! Approaching one of the men, I told him that we were with the Brazilian delegation to the Games and asked him where he was from in Brazil. When he said Curitiba I asked, "Do you know Berek Kriger?"

He replied, "Of course."

Berek, a well known businessman, and two of his kids were at the meet. Explaining our plight, the man was happy to pay our entrance fee, cable car and a soft drink for each. I don't think we could have survived climbing back down the mountain in the 100 plus degree heat.

I was very impressed with the extent that the Jewish state had transformed the desert, and vowed to return some day. Following the meet, Sergio Reitzfeld, my oldest swimmer, traveled with me for one month in Europe, visiting some seven or eight countries. Having been a history major, I was fascinated to see so many of the places I had read about. While on a train going through Germany, I saw a beautiful castle through the window. I turned to the woman sitting across from me in our compartment and asked if she knew the name of this place. It was the famous Heidelburg Castle. I told her we would visit it together the following year.

We exchanged postcards for a year and the next summer I met her at her town outside of Frankfurt to begin a 10-day trip all the way to Switzerland to visit the family where she had been sent during the war along with thousands of other German children to avoid the Allied bombing raids. She planned most of our nightly stops at homes of friends or relatives. One memorable evening we stayed at the home of her cousin in a village in the Black Forest. I don't speak German so, while she and her relatives were catching up in the living room I wandered around the house.

In a bookcase, I noticed a large book that I could understand was a pictorial history of World War II. I browsed through the book and was shocked to find page after page of photos of Hitler being welcomed by cheering crowds in all the countries Germany had conquered. The final and smallest photo was of the gate of the concentration camp in Auschwitz. Rather upset, I walked into the living room and asked if this was the history they taught their children. The cousin replied, shouting, "You don't know what WE suffered during the war. Hitler did many good things for Germany."

I didn't sleep much that night and, at my insistence, we left early the next morning.

By the third year, my Hebraica team had become a national power. We placed 2nd in the short course nationals that winter, though in all fairness, not all of the top teams participated. The following year, our team goal was to win the short course nationals and we had the swimmers to do it. This time, all the top clubs were entered. Our main rival at the time was the club across the street, Pinheiros. We began our taper three weeks from the meet, scheduled for the last weekend in June. That Friday, of the first taper week, I received a call from the swimming federation saying the nationals had been moved to October. I was devastated.

It was so typical of the politicians who ran Brazilian swimming. My kids had trained their hearts out for this meet but now it was rescheduled for the middle of the long course season. What to do? I didn't even notify the swimmers that Friday afternoon and, following the practice, I went to one of Sao Paulo's main streets and just walked trying to think of a solution. The following week was the state short course championships. As I walked, I passed a movie theater showing "The Longest Yard" starring Burt Reynolds. I walked in and though the movie was about an annual football game between inmates and guards at a prison, somehow in my mind, the prisoners became my Hebraica club swimmers and the guards, the Pinheiros team. In the usual Hollywood ending, the prisoners make a miraculous comeback and, for the first time ever, they defeat the guards.

I now had the answer: We had to beat Pinheiros the following weekend at the state meet. The next day, Saturday, I told the swimmers about seeing the movie and knowing that despite not having time to do a proper taper but with the nationals no longer going to happen as scheduled, our focus would now be defeating Pinheiros. I asked the kids to go see the movie and get psyched up.

We rested the following week. When the meet began, the 200 free was the first event. In that kind of situation, everyone is waiting to see how the first swimmer will do. Moises, our first boy, proceeded to drop six seconds and the rout was on. We won by 100 points. What began as a looming disaster turned into one of my most satisfying moments as a coach and a great lesson in the importance of the mental aspect of competition.

Two weeks later, we headed south, to Brazil's traditional South American rival, Argentina, where we had been invited to participate in the Argentine National Championships in Buenos Aires. We arrived in the midst of Argentina's worst hyperinflation. For years, the inflation in Argentina and Brazil would go up and down. With each shift, either the Argentinians would stream into Brazil, bargain hunting, or vice versa. I went to the Adidas factory in BA and bought every single swimsuit they had, for about the equivalent of $3 per suit and sold them for $10 in Brazil. The ever so rude manager of the factory knew exactly what I was going to do but he had no options. On that trip we were paying about $1.50 for a steak dinner with wine and dessert at nice restaurants.

Following our victory at the meet, all the swimmers met for a banquet at the tourist zone of BA which has many restaurants, mostly specializing in chicken dishes. Because of the sudden arrival of so many swimmers, the cooks were hard pressed to meet our order. All the tables had pitchers of wine. While waiting for the chicken to arrive, the dehydrated swimmers attacked the wine on empty stomachs. Soon the swimmers were in all states of inebriation. When the chicken finally arrived, very hot, the famished swimmers cooled it by dipping the pieces into the pitchers of wine. It was a memorable evening, or maybe it wasn't, depending on how much you had to drink.

During my early years of coaching, I had every young coach's dream in my head to someday be an Olympic coach. I thought I had a better chance of attaining it working in South America where the competition wasn't as stiff as in the US. In late 1975, the top five Brazilian coaches and I were summoned to a meeting in Rio, where the Swimming Federation was located. At this meeting, chaired by Rubens Dinard, the president of the Swimming Federation for two decades, we were congratulated for our work and told that for the international meets, including the Olympics, the following year, we would be chosen as national team coaches.

I was pretty excited about the news. The higher you set your hopes, though, the harder you fall. I have never been able to keep my mouth shut when injustice occurs (I guess it is a family trait), especially involving my swimmers. That year, a very good breaststroker transferred to my club. We received assurances from Dinard that she would be eligible for the nationals. Arriving in Rio for the meet, Dinard announced that Miriam could not represent the Hebraica Club. I got in his face but it was useless. Brazil was a military dictatorship and there was nowhere to turn for justice, whether in the sports world or anywhere else.

Dinard had a long memory when it came to perceived threats to his authority and I pretty much burned my bridges on that occasion. He maintained his hold on the federation for many years by buying the votes of the states that had no competitive swimming at election time.

In those days, all newspapers were censored by the military, but each paper had a way of protesting silently. One paper printed blacked-out sections to show how much had been censored. Another, published poems by Brazilian poets in all the spaces that had been censored. All Brazilians are required by law to vote in elections. In protest against the generals who would run for president, many people voted for write-in candidates. Soccer star Pele usually garnered the most write-in votes but Mickey Mouse was a close second.

Arriving in Rio in 1976 for the Age Group Nationals, we found the competition pool closed. We were told that all teams could train at the new Naval Academy pool. Just to be sure, I called the commandant at the Academy to confirm. Receiving his assurance, we piled into the van and drove for an hour to the Academy. On arrival, I was told that, no, we could not use the pool. The new commandant, who had just come on duty, decided not to allow us.

When no one seemed to be looking, I told the swimmers to go ahead and jump in the water. After about two minutes, I noticed someone watching us. He soon disappeared and returned with the goon squad of baton wielding sailors, and gave me 30 seconds to get the kids out of the water or he would unleash his men on them. We got out but when he said the commandant wanted to see me in his office, I took the opportunity to vent. After I thanked him for his support for sports development, I received a tirade that let me know in no uncertain terms that he was in charge and how dare I disobey his orders.

The next day, arriving at the meet venue I was told that the Navy had put in a request to have me deported from Brazil. Fortunately, I had other friends in higher places and they were able to have the order rescinded. I did have the last laugh on that one, though.

Four months later, I received a call from another friend who had organized a meet in Rio with a group of swimmers from Mission Viejo Nadadores. It was to be the official opening of that same Naval Academy pool and I was asked to be the translator for the US team. At the presentation ceremony on the pool deck, I was introduced to the top Brazilian Admiral who thanked me for my help. Standing next to him was the commandant who had reamed me. When introduced to him, I gave him my best smile and said, "So nice to see you again." He was fuming.

When I showed up at the Nadadores hotel in Rio, I asked for the room numbers of the swimmers. Knocking on one of the doors, it was opened up by Jesse Vassallo, the world record holder in the 200 and 400 IM events. There were five or six swimmers in the room, all underage, and quite a few bottles of beer. Someone had discovered that there was no drinking age in Brazil. After I walked in and the door was relocked, there was another knock on the door. Their coach wanted to come in. I held the door shut until the beers were thrown out the window or under the bed. Opening the door, Pat Burch was very suspicious but I said the lock had stuck. Thirty years later, when I called Jesse in Puerto Rico to arrange a masters' clinic, I introduced myself as the guy who saved his ass in Rio.

I met an American woman, a mother of two, who was a swim instructor at another club and we became friends and lovers. She was married to an abusive Brazilian lawyer but she wouldn't leave him and return to the US because by Brazilian law, a wife could only take the children out of the country with the husband's signed permission. I was sort of her crying towel when she was really depressed. One Sunday afternoon she was at my house when a couple of friends showed up. As we smoked a joint and listened to music, Barbara began to feel weird and it took us almost an hour to calm her down. Finally, when she seemed to be ok, we put her in a cab.

Unknown to us, when she arrived home, her husband sensed that something wasn't right and beat out of her where she had been. He then called an acquaintance in the police and gave my name.

The next day, a guy knocked on my door and gave me a summons to appear at the police department office for drug-related cases. I consulted with a neighbor who I knew had a recent close encounter of the same kind and he recommended his lawyer. When I spoke with the lawyer, he told me how much it would cost: part of the fee went to him and part to pay off the police to drop the charges. He would go with me to the precinct and I was to deny everything.

The next day, at the station, the police officer asked me about the party at my house. I didn't know what he was talking about because I still hadn't figured out why I got the summons in the first place. Barbara had been afraid to tell me what had happened with her husband. So, I said there was no party. In the end, I was told that I was being watched and I better keep my nose clean. Six months later, as I was chatting with the multi-millionaire swimming director of my team in his office, the conversation touched on recreational drugs. He shocked me with a comment about what had happened when I was called in by the police.

I asked, "How did you know that?" He replied that the day I was called in, the club lawyer, by coincidence, was at the precinct on other business and was told that a coach from the Hebraica Club was there for questioning. He called the club president who then called the swimming director. I was told that the problem was taken care of and that as long as I didn't do something really stupid, the police wouldn't be bothering me anymore. The implication was that the police had been paid off.

For about a year, Barbara and I, my assistant coaches Oscar and Lula, and Mariana, a young free-spirited Brazilian woman who had just returned to Sao Paulo after a year in the US, had an incredible relationship. We were very close friends and without a jealous bone in our bodies. The three guys often switched off with the two women and occasionally did the threesome thing with varying combinations. One evening, Oscar and I were giving Mariana a massage at my place when the doorbell rang. Oscar was in a better position to answer the door and went, stark naked, to see who was there. I heard a lot of voices and the next thing I knew, a half dozen young people were crowding into the bedroom. It turned out they had knocked on the wrong door but Oscar invited them in and they followed him back to the bedroom. Unfortunately, that ended a very nice evening for the three of us.

My bedroom, both in Porto Alegre and Sao Paulo was unusual. I invited my swimmers over to give me a hand and we painted it all black, everything, including the windows, closet doors and door knobs. Next, we painted hundreds of tiny stars in several colors of phosphorescent paint and in the shapes of constellations and planets. Finally, with the addition of black light and a huge water bed it was the rare woman who could resist the temptation.

Have you ever answered an ad in the personal column? I did, once. I was reading the English language newspaper in Sao Paulo one day, perused the ads and saw one that said something like, "If you want to meet someone who will do anything, write to me, etc." It was crazy enough that it caught my eye and I responded, giving my address. I never got a response.

About a month later, I was home one evening with my assistant coach Lula. We were munching on cheeseburgers and getting ready to try some "lance perfume," a concoction of ether and chloroform which is mixed in a perfume bottle, sprayed on a handkerchief, inhaled and is commonly used to get high during Carnaval. I had never had the courage to try it but someone gave me a bottle and I asked my friend to be there when I used it, just in case.

We had smoked a joint and were enjoying the burgers when the doorbell rang. I opened the door to find a pear-shaped woman I had never seen before. In very British English, she asked if I was going to invite her in and then pushed me aside, sat in a chair and picked up a magazine. I went back into the kitchen where Lula was still eating and whispered to him, "Check it out, who is that?"

He peeked around the corner and shrugged, clueless. Just then, the doorbell rang again. This time it was two friends from my club. We were all sitting in the living room trying to figure out this woman who just sat there reading the magazine. After a couple of minutes, Lula and my two friends got up and went into my bedroom. Soon the smell of the lance perfume wafted out and the sounds of giggling culminated in the three of them walking back into the living room with just their shoes on. I sort of freaked out and went into the other bedroom, slammed the door and sat on the floor just shaking my head and waiting for some sort of disaster to happen. I heard laughing from the other room and opened the door to see the guys crawling on their hands and knees barking at the woman who just sat there calling them "sillies."

I walked in and said, "Ok, put on your clothes, let's go get a beer." They got dressed and we started to leave. The woman just sat there and I said, "This isn't your house. You need to leave as well." She reluctantly followed us downstairs.

When we walked out the building, I yelled to the guys to run back up and we managed to lock the door before the pear was able to get in. I think she hung around a few more minutes before finally leaving. To this day, I can only speculate that she was the woman from the ad but I have never been tempted to try that route again.

In December 1976, I was asked to accompany the University of Indiana swimming team and its legendary coach, Doc Counsilman, during their Christmas training trip to Brazil. What a fabulous opportunity. I translated Doc's talks at clinics and helped with the day-to-day stuff that required a translator. One day, Jim Montgomery, who earlier in the year won gold in the 100 free at the Montreal Olympics, asked me for some help. He was trying to sell the suit he wore when he won Olympic gold to a Brazilian but he couldn't understand what the Brazilian was saying. I facilitated the transaction. Soon after, we sold another suit and then another. I lost track after a while. There were a whole lot of Brazilians with the suit that won the gold medal.

The following summer, I spent a week at Indiana U, picking Doc's brain and watching the taper for the upcoming US Nationals. Montgomery took me around one night to some bars and no sooner did we walk in than the owner would plunk down a pitcher of beer, on the house. The next weekend, Jim won both the 100 and 200 free at the nationals. I always thought about writing an article about the "beer taper" but knew that the American Swimming Coaches Association magazine would never publish it. ASCA's fearless leader, John Leonard, would never publish it.

Doc's son Brian was with the team in Brazil. Brian did a really stupid thing one day in Rio, going up into the *favelas*, the infamous slums, to try and score some grass. Fortunately, he was spotted by some police officers who escorted him back down before he was robbed or worse.

Over the years in South America, strange and often unethical things would happen that to American coaches seem almost unbelievable. At one meet in Porto Alegre, apparently the starter's pistol could not be found. Someone then went home and brought a real gun with live ammo that was used for the meet. After the meet, the swimmers dove in to collect the shell casings in the pool.

At the state indoor short course championships in Sao Paulo one year, someone overlooked telling the pool maintenance man about the meet and hundreds of swimmers had to wait over an hour on Sunday morning until someone went to his house to get the key to open the pool.

Another time, at a 13-14 age group state meet in Sao Paulo, I had just finished chewing out one of my swimmers who had a very late start in his leg of the winning 400 free relay when it was announced that the relay was DQ'd (disqualified). I asked to see the judge's decision and found out that the boy I had just talked to allegedly false started. I then discovered that the judge was from our rival Pinheiros club. When I looked for the judge, someone spotted him running out to his car. A group of swimmers chased him down the street but he had too big of a head start. And his decision, of course, was not overruled.

In 1976, the Uruguay Swimming Federation inaugurated the first indoor 50 meter pool in South America. Teams from the US, Argentina, Taiwan and Brazil were invited for the meet in Maldonado, near the resort area of Punta del Este. I was asked to coach the team representing Southern Brazil. The US squad included Brian Goodell and Mike Bottom.

In the usual rush job to complete the pool on time, the large windows around the pool had just been installed and the putty was not yet dry. The aluminum panels on the roof had not yet been screwed down. The President of Uruguay spoke at the evening inauguration. Soon after his speech, the band, sitting beneath the windows at one side of the pool began playing. Suddenly, a very strong wind came up, blowing so hard that the windows began to bend inward. One of the windows blew out, crashing down on the band and almost severing the legs of one of the members. The aluminum roof panels began to come apart and sailed away with the wind. The lights went out. The stands were full, people began to scream and a stampede ensued. Fortunately, the swimmers were standing under the overhang from the seating area and we just stepped in to a protected room. I felt like an extra in a Hollywood disaster movie. That day's events were moved to the following day.

Olympic trials were held in the spring of 1976. Four guys, three from Sao Paulo and one from Rio combined to make the Olympic cut of 7:55 for the 800 free relay, going 7:53. The next day, the Swimming Federation based in Rio changed the qualifying time just in that one event to 7:51. The Rio swimmer had an individual event qualifying time, so he was still on the team. For several months there were additional qualifying meets and swimmers who had already made the team were expected to swim fast at all these meets. When some coaches protested, Mr. Dinard responded that the business about tapering is just an invention of the coaches; swimmers must swim fast at all meets.

About a month before the Olympics, three female swimmers from Rio went on a TV sports talk show and, crying, said they would not swim anymore unless they were included in the Olympic team. None had come close to qualifying. The next day, they were selected to the team. The three Sao Paulo boys who had qualified stayed home. Needless to say, the performance of the Brazilian team in Montreal was appalling.

For the nationals in early 1977, Mr. Dinard came up with a qualifying system whereby only the top 16 times nationally from the results of the state meets in December could go to nationals. The states were allowed to hold their meets anytime in December of 1976. What happened was, some states held their meets at the beginning of the month, others the second weekend and others on the third. So, you had swimmers waiting more than two weeks after their meet to find out if they had qualified. They didn't know if their season was over or if they should continue to train for the nationals. Furthermore, since there were no qualifying times, it was difficult for coaches to judge how much to taper each swimmer without knowing who the competition was.

In spite of the difficulties, we arrived in Belo Horizonte, the host city, in early 1977, confident that this was our year to win the long course nationals. But it was not meant to be. My top female breaststroker came down with chicken pox just before the qualifying meet and was only able to swim the medley relay. Our women's 400 free relay was DQ'd in prelims for a false start even though all the girls did slow no-risk starts. The nail on the coffin came in the men's 100 free. I had three swimmers in the finals. A swimmer in lane three false started and in the photo taken was clearly under the flags as the other swimmers were leaving the blocks. The false start was so blatant that the swimmers in lanes 2 and 4, both from my Hebraica team, actually stopped when they entered the water. The judge did not call the false start.

Instead of taking 1st, 2nd and 5th in the final, we got 1st, 3rd and 6th. Sergio Reitzfeld in lane 7, who did not see the swimmer entering early, won the race. The boy in lane four, who was the favorite, was so upset that he didn't even qualify for finals in his next race. We ended up losing by four points. Several years later, the swimmer who false started was found shot and killed, his teeth wrenched out, for not paying his debts to drug dealers.

In spite of losing the meet, I qualified 10 swimmers on the national teams going to the Latin Cup, South American Age Group and SA Open Championships Mr. Dinard, once again, opted to ignore me when he appointed the national team coaches so I decided it was time to look for a job in another country. In February, 1977, I told the Hebraica club that I would resign in July, allowing them ample time to find a replacement and offering to help find another US coach, if the club so desired.

I had four swimmers on the Brazilian squad preparing to compete in the Latin Cup in March 1977 in Marseille, France. The swimmers gathered in Rio for a national training camp two weeks before departure for the meet. Sergio Reitzfeld was scheduled to swim the 100 free, both relays and the 200 back in which he finished 2nd at Nationals. Since the first place swimmer in the 100 and 200 back who attended Indiana University had NCAAs that same weekend, Sergio moved up. The Latin Cup allows one swimmer per event per country.

Several days into the camp, I received a call from Sergio. One of the national team coaches from Rio had announced that one of his boys, not on the national team, was looking good, so he decided to hold a time trial in two days to decide who would represent Brazil in the backstroke events. Sergio asked my opinion on what to do and I told him it was a sham. After the national team is already chosen, this guy decides to have another time trial which would impact the taper of those going to the meet. Sergio already had the 100 free and both relays so we decided to leave it at that. The boy who was scheduled to swim the 100 back also refused to take part in the trial.

The Rio kid swam alone and though he went considerably slower than the two qualified swimmers, he was selected to swim both backstroke events. Unbelievable!! But it gets better. In the team hotel, one day before leaving for Rome, Sergio was told that he would not be getting on the plane. He had been kicked off the team for insubordination for not participating in the time trial. All the swimmers were summoned to a meeting and warned that if anyone protested the decision, they would also be kicked out. Sergio was one of the swimmers who had qualified for the Olympic relay the previous year and lost his opportunity then, too. He finished the short course season and stopped swimming. You can just imagine the frustration of seeing this happen to your swimmer and knowing there is not a goddamn thing you can do about it.

The weeks went by in the countdown towards my departure from Brazil. I went to Venezuela to visit my former swimmers and received a job offer from the Hebraica club in Caracas whose sports director I had met some years earlier in Argentina. I was selected to go with the Brazil team to the Maccabiah Games that summer before leaving for good. On June 6th, just as practice was ending, I noticed a messenger boy coming towards the pool from the sports office. I turned to my assistant coach, "Oscar, we are about to be fired."

On the other side of the pool, the swimming director was herding the swimmers to the pool office. The messenger boy asked us to go to the sports director's office.

Upon entering, we were asked to be seated and told that the Chief of Police of Sao Paulo, a city of 12 million people at that time, had visited the club the previous day, and informed the director that Oscar and I were involved with drugs. If we agreed to resign and leave the country in a timely fashion, everything would be okay. If not, the club could not be responsible for our safety. It was absurd to make the claim about the chief of police's visit but, in a military dictatorship, you sign the paper.

As this was taking place, the swimming director was telling the swimmers in the pool office that Rick and Oscar were involved in something so bad that he could not tell them what it was, and that we would no longer be working there. The following day, I went to the US Consulate in Sao Paulo and told the vice consul what had happened and how the police had been paid off three years before. Her advice, "Get out of Dodge. These people can pay to have you disappear just as they paid to have you left alone. This is a military dictatorship. You have no rights."

I put out the word to the swimmers to meet at my apartment and told them what had actually happened. We remain great friends to this day.

So, that is the end of the Brazilian chapter of my coaching career. I have gone back to Brazil many times since to give clinics, visit my former swimmers who are like family to me, and to discover new places in one of the most beautiful countries in the world. A year after I left, the Hebraica team slipped from 2nd place to 13th in the nationals and has never recovered its place as a national swimming power. I will admit that I did get some satisfaction from that.

Chapter V
Return to Venezuela—A Bad Move, 1977-78

I returned to Caracas in August, 1977, hired by the Hebraica Club, another beautiful Jewish Community Center with a mediocre swim team. As in Sao Paulo, one of my conditions was a commitment by the club to open its doors to non-Jewish swimmers. Within weeks, a dozen of Venezuela's top swimmers, some of whom had trained with me years before, and others attracted by my reputation for having a great rapport with the swimmers, had joined my new team.

We began preparing for the December national championships. Every week, I would attend a meeting of the swimming federation to monitor the transfer process of my new swimmers. I was given absolute assurance that all requirements had been met. With the less experienced Jewish swimmers now full of confidence from training with their new national level companions, we arrived in Maracay for a five-day meet expecting some great swims.

On the evening of our arrival, I went to the opening congress of coaches and delegates and was told that a secret meeting of all the clubs, except ours, had been held and a decision was made that my transfer swimmers would be relegated to the consolation final heats and could not win medals or score points. It was just another memorable example of the political slime that permeates sports in the third world. I went back to the hotel and called the swimmers together, explained the situation and told them that we have no choice but to show these assholes what we are made of. "You are ready to swim fast and you will swim fast."

At prelims the next morning we had some excellent results. When we arrived for the finals, none of my swimmers were listed in the heat sheet for consolations. I demanded that the officials redo the heat sheet and they were inserted after a one hour delay, but only in lanes one or eight. Again, I complained. How could the fastest swimmers be in lanes one and eight? I was told that all the lanes were the same. If I didn't like it, they wouldn't swim at all.

We had some great swims that evening except for one nasty incident. In the boys 10 and under 50 m breast, our entry was already a body length ahead at the 15 meter mark when the false start rope was dropped on his head. Of course, he stopped. The rope was immediately lifted and the other swimmers went on to finish the race. When I protested, I was told the boy could swim by himself at the end of the meet!

The next day, in the girls 11-12 200 IM, one of my girls won the consolation heat by almost two body lengths. When the results were announced, she had been placed 2nd. I ran up to the announcer's table demanding to see the place judges' cards. They had all been erased and the other girl's name inserted in first. My limitless patience was beginning to run out. Later that session, the announcer called event 30 to the blocks, the open 100 free, but event 29 hadn't been called yet. I ran to the announcer's table to point out the error but was told to mind my own business. The start was given while my swimmer was still pulling off his jacket.

When we arrived the next morning, day four, I was informed that another secret meeting had been held and it was decided that there would be no more consolation finals for the rest of the meet. My limit was exceeded. I went up to the president of the Federation, put my arm around his shoulder and said, very calmly, "Miguel, during my 12 years coaching in South America, I have seen many lousy officials but you are definitely the worst."

He yelled, "You are suspended for two years!"

I replied, "And, furthermore, you are a *juevon* (asshole)."

He then suspended me for five years. At that point, many of our parents and swimmers came down on deck and shoving matches ensued with the officials. Two of the top clubs withdrew from the meet and went home.

Back in Caracas, shortly after the Nationals debacle, I was on deck, at practice, preparing for an upcoming meet in Trinidad when a man I hadn't seen before called me over to the stands.

"Who are those dark skinned swimmers (referring to the non-Jewish ones)?" he asked. I replied that they were the scholarship swimmers.

A couple of days passed by and I had forgotten about him when I received a letter from the club advising me that I had one month to dismiss the non-Jewish swimmers. I was appalled. I had recently received an offer from the Italian-Venezuelan club but had declined. I called them that evening to see if the offer was still open and would they accept my swimmers, too. The answer was yes.

The next day I had a meeting with the swimmers and explained what was going on and that I would never work in a place that discriminated for whatever reason. I told them that everyone who wished could join me the following week at the Italian club but to keep it quiet until after that weekend's meet in Trinidad. No one said a thing and the next week I switched clubs. Even some of the Jewish kids came with me. The Hebraica team slipped back into mediocrity.

Over the Christmas break that year, 1977, I went to Cuba and gave a clinic for the Cuban coaches at the National Sports Institute. It was a great experience. The Cubans treated me like royalty. It was so refreshing after what I had just been through in Venezuela. One Sunday afternoon in Havana, I was walking around seeing the sights when I spotted a good size stadium in the distance. I went over to check it out and heard cheering inside. Going up to the guard at an entrance I asked what sport was taking place and he told me it was a baseball game. When I asked how much it cost to enter, he said, "We don't charge for sports events in Cuba."

He could tell by my accent that I was a foreigner and when he asked me where I was from I responded, just a bit apprehensively, the US. He began shouting to some people nearby, "American, American."

They rushed over and escorted me to front row box seats, bought me a couple of beers and we ended up going drinking after the game. Later, I hopped on a tourist bus to hitch a ride back to the hotel district. Taking the only empty seat and with my Indiana Swimming t-shirt on, I said hello to the guy in the next seat. He asked where I got the shirt. "From Doc Counsilman, the Indiana coach," I replied. He told me to say hi for him the next time I saw Doc. He had been Doc's roommate in college!

My last night in Cuba, I was taken to dinner at a very fancy restaurant outside of Havana, in what used to be a sugar factory. I was driven to the restaurant with the presidents of the Swimming Federation and the Sports Institute, and was amazed when the driver of the Sports Institute car also sat down with us for dinner. Anywhere else in South America he would have waited in the parking lot for us to finish. When I asked him about this, he said that before the revolution he was an illiterate peasant farmer. Now, he could read and write, his kids were both in school and he had a small apartment, which he took me to see on the way to the airport the next day. He was very proud of what the revolution had accomplished. It was a very different perspective from what we had heard from our government.

In Venezuela, as in many Latin American countries, the equivalent of our debutante balls is held for upper class girls on their 15th birthday. I wasn't really aware how fancy these affairs are. When one of my girls, Ana, invited me to her party, I showed up in slacks and a nice shirt, about as much as I ever dress up. I arrived at her building with my invitation but the armed guard at the door wouldn't let me in. When Ana appeared on the balcony of her apartment on the 3rd floor, I shouted up to her and she told the guard to let me in. I took the elevator and quickly understood why the guard's reluctance. I received quite the shock when the elevator door opened and I gazed upon this spectacle of men in tuxedos and women in floor length gowns. I felt really out of place but Ana led me in and introduced me to a few people, plus, all her swimming buddies were there. The daughter of the President of Venezuela was there, too. When the band began to play, I probably had the best time of anyone, dancing without the formal attire to cramp my style.

Back in Venezuela to start my new job in January, I was informed that my nemesis, Miguel, had lost his bid for reelection as president of the Swimming Federation and the new president, a crotchety old journalist, had revoked my suspension.

The next goal for my swimmers was the qualifying meet for the South American Senior Championships, to be held in May in my old stomping grounds of Guayaquil, Ecuador. When the order of events for the trials was published, there were back-to-back events that were on different days at the SA Championships. I pointed this out to the federation saying, "You are shooting yourselves in the foot. Why propose an order of events that is only going to make it more difficult for our swimmers to qualify?" Needless to say, I was ignored.

After the trials, the team representing Venezuela was chosen. Six of the 10 swimmers were from my club. By the rules, I had to be named the national coach. Well, guess what? Someone else with one swimmer was chosen. The club decided to pay my expenses to accompany the swimmers to Guayaquil. I arrived two days before the team to visit with old friends and received a deck pass from the Ecuadorians.

I had two girls and four boys on that team. When they arrived, one of the girls called me and said she had brought my mail. I dropped by their room to pick it up and was introduced to the chaperone. Subsequently, the Venezuelan officials accused me of having sex with the girls when I was there. The chaperone never admitted she was in the room with us.

When I went to the pool later that afternoon to see the swimmers at their practice time, the kids all came over to say hello. The Venezuelan team delegate called the swimmers away and warned them that if any of them was so much as seen talking to me, they would be sent back to Venezuela on the next flight. I spent the meet up in the stands.

Returning to Venezuela the following week, all four boys received two-year suspensions. To this day, no reason has ever been given. I decided it was time to return to the United States. Four of my swimmers came with me and I found teams for them, either with me or elsewhere in the Midwest. I had been recruiting swimmers for Southern Illinois University for a decade and I asked Al Smith, the men's coach, if he could come up with something for me at SIU. Al arranged for me to be an assistant coach with his Salukis and head coach of the local age group team, Jackson County YMCA.

Chapter VI
SIU before Title IX, 1978-80

I had attended SIU in 1966, my freshman year, and swam on the team. Carbondale is way off the beaten path but a succession of good coaches had kept the men's team competitive for 20 years. I arrived one day before classes began in the fall of 1978. Al found a rickety old trailer, the last place available, for me to live in. The plan was to begin work on a Masters degree in PE, as well as coach the two teams. I brought three swimmers to SIU with me—a boy from Argentina and a girl from Venezuela, as well as a Venezuelan boy for my age group team.

It was tough being back in the classroom after 12 years, and with my coaching duties, I must admit, focusing on the classroom was not a priority.

That fall, our traditional first meet was the Rolla Relays in Missouri. We drove out for the meet; Al and I were staying with the Rolla coach and when we arrived a bit tired and thirsty, we asked for a beer.

"No beer," he replied.

"How about a soft drink or iced tea?"

"No, I'm a Mormon," he said.

We went out for a beer.

After the meet, we stopped off at the Current River for the traditional canoe trip. The SIU men's team was an interesting bunch. It consisted of a large group of Born Again Christians, a band of stoners and a few non-aligned swimmers. When we arrived at the river, the Christians got in their canoes and raced down the river. The stoners had a toke and drifted down the river, arriving long after, to the taunts of the Christians.

Al was masterful in dealing with those guys. I remember an incident where he was analyzing the race of Ben, one of the top swimmers, and pointing out where he could have improved his time, when the swimmer said, "No, Al, God didn't want me to win."

If it had been me, I probably would have strangled the guy. I later had a conversation with Ben to find out what it was he believed in and he said that if you don't take Jesus Christ as your savior, you go to hell. I asked, "What about people who lead good lives, helping others?"

"No," he said, "they must take JC as their savior."

Then I asked, "What about a two-year old who dies in a car accident?"

He stopped to think and said he would consult on that one and get back to me. When I asked him about it the next day, he couldn't remember that part of our conversation.

Ben would hold Sunday evening bible classes to indoctrinate the freshmen. His most notable conversion was SIU's best swimmer, a very versatile West Coast swimmer who was a multiple event NCAA finalist anwhodwho briefly held the American record in the 200 fly. He works for NASA now, a scary thought.

For the next couple of years after I left SIU, I would return for two weeks in the summer to help Al run a swim camp for teams I recruited from South America. One summer, I ran into John and decided to find out why a guy who was so happy-go-lucky in his freshman year could make such an abrupt about-face and get involved in fundamental Christian beliefs. His response was to tell me three stories. Ben had convinced him by relating the first two incidents by relating the first two which had supposedly happened to Ben.

One day, Ben left swimming practice with an aching muscle. He went to the trainer to get an ice pack and was told there weren't any. Walking back to the dorm, Ben prayed for an ice pack and, lo and behold, one appeared on the sidewalk in front of him! Whew, I don't know about the ice pack, but I could have used an ice cold beer after that story.

Next, one summer, Ben and some "Christian" friends were camping in a wilderness area in Canada when suddenly, a storm blew in. They decided to sit it out in their tent but the high winds broke the wooden tent poles. They decided to pray for help and, lo and behold, a little old man walked out of the forest with a bag of steel tent poles for them. Damn, another cold beer, please.

"So," I said, "that's all good, John, but those are Ben's stories. How about you? Did you just decide to change your life based on what others told you?"

"No," he replied, "The summer after my freshman year, while at the national training camp, I received a call from my girlfriend telling me that she had missed her period. I wanted to do the right thing so, that night, for the first time in my life, I prayed. And lo and behold, the next day she called me, 'My period came!'" Hey, can't argue with that, can you?

In December the women's coach at SIU was fired. She was East German, a former swimmer who treated her swimmers as she had been treated under the Communist system. By December, only three women remained on the team. Al spoke with the women's athletic director, Dr. West, who looked exactly like the Wicked Witch of the West from 'Wizard of Oz', and I was appointed to finish out the year, but without a salary.

At that time, before Title IX, the women's coaches earned about 50% of the men's coaches' salaries and had about a fourth of the scholarships. Al was kind enough to give me an NCAA scholarship that semester to help me pay my rent. He got in trouble for doing that but I don't recall it being anything serious.

Al did get on my case once when he found out I was dating one of the lifeguards at the Rec Center. "Powers, you can't date the lifeguards."

I said, "No, YOU can't date them, I'm single."

Using my international connections, that fall, I began to prepare a Christmas training trip for the combined SIU teams. I thought it would be a really cool experience if I could arrange a trip to Cuba and the Cubans were receptive, especially after the US table tennis team had opened the door a bit. Everyone was excited and the media gave us some good coverage. We chartered a flight out of Miami.

Four days before our scheduled departure, I received a call at 10 PM from someone from the Cuban Foreign Ministry explaining that we must cancel our trip because there was no housing available. The Swim Federation had hoped to find housing but our trip was right in the middle of the festivities for the 10th Anniversary of the Cuban revolution and everything was booked. I was so pissed. The next day, I called everyone I could think of, including friends in Washington, but no one really had any leverage with the Cubans. So Al decided we would train in Florida where the team was headed originally to catch the flight to Cuba.

But on Christmas Eve, two days before departure, I had an emergency appendectomy and didn't make the trip. How ironic. There are two things I remember about my three-day hospital stay. On Christmas Day, I was supposed to be on an IV and no solid foods. At about 4 PM, a group of my swimmers arrived with a gym bag. In it were plates of turkey, stuffing, desserts and a bottle of wine. When no one was looking, I feasted. A week later, getting the stitches out, my doctor expressed his sympathy for me on Christmas, having to chow down on the IV. When I told him what I had eaten, he was aghast. "You could have burst the internal stitches and died,." Oh, well, it sure tasted good at the time.

The second dumb thing I did in the hospital was trying to have sex with my girlfriend who was visiting from Florida and who was returning the next day with the SIU team. The nurse on duty promised not to let anyone disturb us and we gave it a try but it felt like my external stitches were about to burst, so, we gave up on that idea.

Then, driving my stick shift home from the hospital after being told not to drive for a few days, I got rear ended at a stop sign. The front bumper of the car that hit me went under my rear bumper and a screw on it went into a hole in my bumper. It took almost an hour and two tow trucks to free the cars. Meanwhile, I was standing in the snow, freezing in a t-shirt, only to arrive home to find that the heating system in my ancient trailer wasn't working. Didn't mommy tell us there would be days like these?

When I took over the women's team at semestral break, I was able to convince several of the swimmers to rejoin the team. I only had a couple of months left to get them back in shape before the conference meet at Illinois State University. Prior to that, we participated in an invitational meet at Indiana University. With only a couple weeks training, I didn't expect much from my swimmers. Returning from Indiana, the sports reporter for the school paper asked me how the girls did. I replied, "We had some good times but they weren't in the pool." The athletic director wasn't pleased. Those witches have no sense of humor.

At conference champs, the girls swam exceptionally well. We lost the meet to the host team on the basis of three DQs. Two girls qualified for nationals. On the way home on the interstate, a semi flipped over during a freak snow storm, blocking the highway. About two thousand people were stranded. After several hours without food, we traded a couple of beers left over from the previous night's party for a case of French onion dip from the truck behind us. Not a good move. About an hour after eating the dip with our fingers, everyone began to fart. It was nasty.

The National Guard finally got to us and took everyone to a small town nearby where we were given blankets and slept on the floor of the elementary school. The local townspeople were wonderful, bringing hot soup and sandwiches for everyone and offering their telephones for people to call their families.

When I decided in December to take over the women's team without getting paid, it was with the agreement that the permanent coach for the following year would be appointed by the end of February. This was to allow time to recruit for the next season. The athletic director dragged out the process until the end of April, by which time virtually all the decent swimmers I had hoped to sign had gone elsewhere. I basically picked up some leftovers, borderline academics, an alcoholic, a kleptomaniac and a girl who got pregnant and dropped out of school soon after the season started.

Over the summer break, I went to Mexico City and set up our Christmas training trip for 1979. This time, it all came together. We were hosted by the largest Mexican team, trained for one week at the Olympic training center, and then went to Guadalajara to compete against the Mexican National Team at the new 50 meter University of Guadalajara pool. It was a very exciting three-day meet.

After the first day, the Mexicans were well ahead and the newspapers headlined: "Mexico trouncing US." After the second day, we had recovered some ground. It all came down to the two medley relays at the end of the third day. The women swam first and though we had lost every individual 100 stroke race, the girls pulled together and dropped an average of 2.5 seconds to upset the Mexican team. The men iced it with another victory and we celebrated into the night. A few worms were eaten that night from the bottom of tequila bottles.

The Mexican team generously paid all our expenses except for our flight from Chicago. One morning, while we were still at the Olympic training center, several of the girls approached me. "We have been missing money and jewelry from our luggage and suspect that Alice has been stealing our stuff. When she was in the bathroom this morning, we found everything in her bag."

I asked them to let me talk to Alice first before we would decide what to do. Alice admitted everything, agreed to return everything and go for counseling when we returned to SIU. In return, I said I wouldn't tell her parents. Back at school, I scheduled a meeting with a counselor. But when I called Alice to remind her about an hour before the session, she said she wasn't going and that she had never stolen anything. The deal was off. So I called her father, a dean at the university, and told him all that had transpired.

He said, "Funny thing, now I know why my wife's jewelry has been vanishing." Alice had also stolen from her roommate at the dorm. She flunked out that semester but eventually got her life back together, re-enrolled and graduated from college.

With only eight eligible women on the team in my second season, I had decided early on that SIU wasn't working out. Making only $700 a month and having to coach the age group team just to make ends meet was taking the fun out of coaching. From mid-October to mid-April, I had a meet every single weekend, without a day-off. That second season culminated in the state meet at Western Illinois University. Always having to live frugally on our limited budget, instead of housing in a motel, I had arranged for us to stay at a dorm on campus where the rooms were much cheaper.

At 2:30 AM on the night before the meet began, the fire alarms went off in the dorm. There actually was a fire. Everyone had to evacuate the dorm and stand outside in the snow for almost two hours before being allowed to return. A grumpy and tired group of swimmers went to the pool the next morning and didn't swim well. But one of the girls and one of the divers, did qualify for nationals in Vegas and we packed our bags. Two more girls went, too, paying their own way to watch the meet.

I was able to get us one of those Las Vegas package deals. Eight days with hotel was cheaper than four, and since it was over spring break, the athletic director gave us the thumbs up. By the third day, we were done swimming. It was all gravy after that. We discovered that every hotel/resort will give you a free mixed drink. It was fun trying to reach the other end of the strip still able to walk. Knowing it was my last meet with them, the girls gave me a nice present, a collective massage.

Sao Paulo state in Brazil and Illinois had an exchange program called Partners of the Americas. I was invited to give two clinics in Sao Paulo and, with the athletic director's blessing, went there for a month after the nationals. On my return, Dr. West informed me that I wouldn't be paid for the month I was gone. This was my reward for working for free the first season.

I had the last laugh, as usual. My roommate, Joe Lynch, and I shared a nice house on the edge of Carbondale that second year where we had lots of parties, lots of good times. Joe was divorced and would occasionally bring his six-year-old daughter for the weekend. One day, we were shopping at a grocery store during the holidays after watching 'The Wizard of Oz' on TV when, suddenly, his daughter screamed, "The Wicked Witch!!" She had spotted Dr. West coming down the aisle. We picked her up and ran around to the next aisle, laughing until our tears streamed down.

The other half of my employment in Carbondale consisted of coaching a team of about 40 kids at the YMCA. Over that two-year period, I brought over half a dozen Brazilian and Venezuelan swimmers and housed them with the local kids. One of the swimmers was from a wealthy family. During the first year, he lived with a family, but the second, his mom came and rented a condo, bought two cars and spent the year with us. She was an extremely generous woman and often treated all the swimmers to a nice meal.

We participated in the Illinois Regional YMCA championships in April 1979 in Belleville, across the Mississippi from St. Louis. The boys competed on Saturday, the girls on Sunday. After Saturday's events, one of the coaches invited me over to her motel room across the street. When I knocked on the door, it opened but the room lights were out. I could see five or six couples making out on the beds, chairs and floor. The coach asked one of the couples to leave the bed and pulled me on to it. As we began to kiss, someone whispered in her ear and she said, "Wait a minute." She rose and went into the bathroom with one of the girls. I heard some arguing but soon she was back and we resumed where we had left off.

Immediately, I noticed the kiss had changed. I turned on the bed lamp and saw that one of her girls had taken her place. I asked, "What in the hell are you doing?"

She replied, "My coach is married and shouldn't be making out with you but I didn't think it was fair that you be alone." She must have been about 15. I was out that door before you could wink an eye.

We drove up to Chicago in early 1980 to participate in the Illinois State Junior Olympic meet. After prelims one day, I dropped the kids at the hotel and took my Mom, who still lived in Chicago, out to lunch. Arriving back at the hotel at about 3 PM, I was parking my car when the hotel manager came out and asked me to come to his office. I walked in to find my five swimmers seated in the office. The manager told me how the kids had caused a fire that burned about 15 feet of carpet in the corridor outside their rooms. He was ready to call the police but I asked him if we could settle it by paying the damages and he agreed. I paid and took the kids to my room to find out what had happened.

They agreed to pay me back and I promised not to tell their parents. What occurred was that the other boys wanted to play a trick on the Venezuelan boy. One of them shit in a dish, covered it with toilet paper, lit it and put it in front of his door. They knocked on his door and waited in the next room. Bernie came out, stamped on the fire to put it out, got his shoe covered with shit but also set the carpet on fire. Not the brightest kids on the block.

In the spring of 1980, we had a dual meet with a team from the St. Louis area. I had rented a bus and went to the meet with about 40 swimmers. I didn't allow parents to travel with the team. On the way back on Sunday evening, I sat at the front of the bus chatting with the driver. The older kids were sitting at the back and were unusually quiet but I was tired and was grateful for the silence.

When we arrived at the parking lot of the "Y" in Carbondale where the parents were waiting to pick up their children, the older swimmers staggered off the bus, drunk. I was extremely angry because I had always trusted them to abide by the rules and it was the first time they had broken that trust. The next day, I received a call from the club president, the Lutheran pastor in town, requesting my presence at the Wednesday board meeting. He enumerated seven or eight topics to be discussed, with the Belleville trip mentioned last.

I showed up at the meeting and was told by the president that the JCY kids were always exemplary students and role models, etc, and what was going on now? I responded that their exemplary children planned the incident, stealing liquor from their parents to consume on the return trip and that I was as upset as anyone. The pastor ranted a bit about the moral decline of young people and I left. I went over to my girlfriend's house, still pissed off about the situation. While discussing the incident with the swimmers, I noticed a photo of the pastor on her bookcase. "Why do you have a photo of Duane, Beth?"

She replied that she sang in the church choir.

"So, why do you have a photo of Duane?"

She said that he had counseled her when she was going through her divorce.

"So, why do you have a photo of Duane?" She finally admitted that while counseling her, he was also bonking her.

I cracked up. The sanctimonious bastard! I had eaten dinner at his house a couple of times over the two years I was there. He had a portrait of himself in the living room with Christ in the background and the caption, "As was He, so do I try to be." Yeah, right.

About 15 years later, when I was back in Carbondale, I called his house to see if I could locate his kids. His wife answered and informed me that they were now divorced and she was the President of the local lesbian organization. I was so shocked that I forgot to ask about the kids.

Over the summer, I received an offer to return to Ecuador to coach the exclusive Quito Tenis Club in the capital city in the Andes Mountains.

Chapter VII
Ecuador, Part II, 1980-81

It was going to be an interesting experience living in Quito. The people from the Andes region despise the people from the coast, where I had lived before. Each says their version of Spanish is the correct one. In addition, Quito is over 8,000 feet about sea level and the opportunity to train at that altitude would be a challenge.

A few days after I arrived, I was on deck when a waiter from the bar on the pool balcony yelled that I had a phone call. I took the call and a woman said that she used to date the former American coach and would like to invite me for dinner at her restaurant. Sure, why not?

We met the next evening at her Bavarian-style restaurant and while sipping a beer and waiting for the meal, she reached across the table, placed her hand on mine and said, "I don't want you dating any other women, and my brother is an army officer."

I almost lost it, wanting to fall on the ground laughing but somehow, I held my composure and got through dinner. We went to my apartment for the after-dinner roll in the hay and off she went. The next night, I was sleeping when the phone rang at about midnight. I staggered into the living room to grab the phone and when I picked up the receiver, a familiar voice started yelling, "So who is there with you? I told you no other women!" I told her never to do that again, that I had practice the next morning at 6 AM. For the next three nights, the scene was repeated until I told her to fuck off and never bother me again.

I was invited by a neighboring club to bring a group of my swimmers for a demonstration at the Sunday inauguration of their new swimming pool. During the demonstration, I kept getting the "look" from a lovely young lady in a black bikini. As I took a stroll around the club garden, she passed me and slipped a piece of paper into my hand with a name and telephone number. I called that evening and she asked if I could meet her at her father's office on Monday morning.

I said, "How about dinner?" No, she said, her father's office, across the street from the Congress building. Always ready for something new, I showed up at 10 AM and knocked on the door of a law office on the fourth floor. She opened the door into a short hallway and began to kiss me. Hell, I couldn't see if anyone was in the office so I said, "Hang on a minute. Where is your father?"

She locked the outer door, pulled me into the office, put the couch pillows on the floor and as she stripped, said, "We have one hour." Not one to be checking the clock while having a good time, I was suddenly reminded that her father would be arriving any minute. Talk about a quick dress and out the door in record time. I never saw her again. Her father didn't allow her to date and that one-hour fling was cutting it too close.

The Quito Tenis Club was hosting an ATP Tennis Tour Championship and asked for my help in ordering the equipment needed for the event from the US. I was able to get some good discounts and they were very happy. When my buddy from Carbondale, Joe Lynch, wanted to come for a visit, I told the club that he was the sales rep for the tennis equipment company in the US and they should pay his way to come down and check it out. So, Joe got a free vacation trip to Ecuador.

A day after his arrival, we were on our way to Guayaquil for a swim meet. One of the swimmers' drivers picked us up in a vintage Ford Mustang. On the way to the airport, driving down the busiest street in Quito, an Indian with a basket of onions on his head ran through the bumper-to-bumper traffic and proceeded to put his head through our windshield. Joe was freaking out in the back seat but the Indian rolled off the car, picked up his onions and continued on his merry way.

The club would pay me a bonus of five cents for each tenth of a second that the swimmers improved their best times at meets. At that meet, I put a bunch of kids in the 1500 free. What with the altitude training, some of them dropped more than a minute. I made a bundle. Following the meet, Joe and I headed to a lovely beach front fishing village where one of my former swimmers had a house. She was going back to visit her family over the Christmas holidays so we had the place to ourselves. It was a simple place. We had two bedrooms with mattresses on the floor. The second morning, I was awakened by Joe's screams. I rushed to his room to find a 400 pound monster pig standing next to his mattress. We were able to shoo it away, finally.

The afternoons we spent going out with the fishermen and buying their lobsters for $1 apiece. Joe is a gourmet cook, so we feasted. The day before returning to Guayaquil to catch the plane back to Quito, we checked to see what time the morning bus would depart. The next morning, we arrived at 8 AM for the 8:30 departure, just to be sure. When the bus still hadn't arrived by nine, I asked someone, only to find out it had left at 7:30. So we decided to hitch a ride. When an old truck came by and stopped, we were told to get in the back. We threw in our bags and climbed over the side only to settle into the slime of a fish truck. It wasn't an easy ride since we had to stand up the whole way trying not to slide as the truck bounced on the rutted road. Our shoes and bags were pretty much trashed by the time we got to Guayaquil and, boy, did some noses wrinkle up as we walked into our fancy hotel.

In a taxi the next day, we passed a couple of women in another car who agreed to meet that night at a disco. I found out that one of them would be coming up to Quito the next week to visit her aunt and invited her to dinner while she was there. We made the inevitable pilgrimage to my water bed after dinner and, at one point, completely naked and in each other's arms, she jumped up and said, "What kind of girl do you think I am?" as she got dressed and left. I'm still trying to figure that one out but I have a theory that it has to do with the altitude. Lack of oxygen to the brain, maybe?

One morning, on the way to the pool at 5:30 AM, after being picked up by the father of one of the swimmers, we were the only vehicle on a wide street when an Indian woman, her head wrapped in a poncho, ran across the street right in front of our car. We hit her at 50 mph and she somersaulted through the air. As the driver slammed on his brakes, I began to open my door. He grabbed me and sped off with his daughter crying in the back seat. He said that no matter who is at fault, the driver will be jailed if he hits an Indian, so you don't stop. They come down from the mountain villages and don't have a clue about crossing streets.

We had a great meet at the trials for the South American Age Group Championships in Guayaquil. The Ecuadorian team was selected and though I should have been one of the national coaches, again I was ignored. The club paid my way to Medellin, Columbia for the meet. We were ready to leave for the pool the first morning and found that the Ecuadorian head coach, who was stinking drunk the night before, never made it to the pool. So, ironically, I ended up coaching the whole team that day. Our team bus had a military escort everywhere we went due to the threat of kidnapping from drug dealers.

During my last year in Sao Paulo, I had a 15-year-old Israeli swimmer on my team. His father, who was teaching Israeli dances at the Hebraica club, had brought the family to Brazil for that year. We stayed in touch for the next couple of years and at one point, in the summer of 1980, before going to Ecuador, I decided to visit Israel again. His coach arranged a clinic for me at the Israeli Sports Institute. After the clinic, several coaches invited me to visit their teams and, so I was able to see quite a bit of the country and even made it to Egypt for a week.

Crossing the Sinai Desert by bus, we reached the Egyptian border. Most of the Sinai had already been returned to Egypt. At the crossing, I met a tall blonde German woman and we decided to travel together. She had an Egyptian friend in Munich who had given her a package to take to her family, just outside Cairo. We went to the suburban train station to catch the train to visit the family. The station was packed with thousands of people on the platform. Earlier in the day, a train had derailed and traffic had been halted for hours. Finally, a train arrived and we were shoved in by the mob, not having any idea which train it was. Packed tighter than sardines in a can, we couldn't even lift our arms.

My friend then told me that the guys around her were squeezing her butt and legs. We began to yell and the conductor in our car was passed over the heads of the crowd to where we were stuck. Here he was, being held up in the air by numerous hands, shouting in Arabic to the guys around us. They actually behaved for the remainder of the trip and, miraculously, we were on the right train and reached our destination, a terrible slum of tenements, mostly with broken windows, piles of trash in the streets, and beggars everywhere.

Finding the right building, she knocked on the door and a woman opened it. She gave her a note in Arabic. The woman embraced us, proceeded to call everyone within hearing distance, sat us down for tea and began to cook, probably the worst meal I had ever eaten. I don't know how I didn't puke on the floor. At about 10 PM, the father said: "Go fast, last train," and we happily rushed back to the station. The two-car train was ready to go. We ran inside the first car, closely followed by a guy who said, "Come, Come" and brought us into the forward car. He was the driver and spoke about two words of English. As we left the station, he lit up his hash pipe and we buzzed on back to Cairo, stopping at each station for a cold beer supplied by one of his friends. He let us drive the train, too. No wonder the trains derail.

Before departing Quito, I had the opportunity to visit the Galapagos Islands. One of the club members was a travel agent and he managed to get me a package tour to go as an Ecuadorian, rather than a foreigner, which meant a 50% discount. I went during the off-season and had a cabin to myself on the small (90 passenger) cruise ship. The ship had four guides, one for each major language. The English-speaking guide, an American, was a former Standard Oil executive who, tired of the corporate world, had been living on the boat for five years enjoying his passion, the wildlife of the islands.

I received a couple of job offers from Israeli teams that year and eventually decided to try that country which had fascinated me on my two previous trips. So, in the summer of 1981, I resigned from the Quito Tenis club and took about 20 swimmers back to the US with me for the SIU swim camp. Since they were all younger swimmers, the families asked me to take care of their money. I had 20 envelopes, each with

$1,000 in cash which I doled out each time they had to pay for something. What a hassle! I paired off the 13 and over swimmers with the 12 and under and miraculously no one got lost.

Following the camp, I took the team to Miami to compete in a meet with teams from 20 Latin American and Caribbean countries. After the meet, I went over to the Venezuelan swimmers' post-meet party in their hotel rooms. In walked Ana, one of the swimmers who I had sent to the States when I left Venezuela. She was living at Coach Jack Nelson's house and, though she was no longer swimming, she came to the party to see her friends. I was seated on one of the beds with a drink. Ana came straight over and sat on my lap.

"What a surprise," she said. We soon knew what was going to happen next and slid under the bedcover. With the cover up to our waists, we slipped off our shorts and caressed each other under the blanket. The room was packed with swimmers and parents. At one point, someone said that they were out of ice. I yelled, "Ten dollars to the first person who brings the ice."

Exactly as I had hoped, everyone ran out to find ice. I quickly locked the door. By the time they came back I think they had figured out what was going on and for the next half hour, people were knocking on the door and both walls from the rooms on either side. Ana and I decided it was quieter in the shower. When we finally emerged from the room, we were greeted by cheers from the crowd waiting to get back in. A week later, I went to Israel.

Chapter VIII
Israel, Broken Promises in the Promised Land, 1981-83

In the fall of 1981, I arrived in Israel thinking that this just might be the place where I would want to stay for a long time. I was hired by a club called Geshom Hapoel based on the Kibbutz Givat Haim Ichoud, about a 10-minute drive from the crossroads junction town of Hadera. For those unfamiliar with the Kibbutzim, they are, basically, socialistic agricultural communities first founded in the early years of the 20th century. On the kibbutz, you are assigned a job and given an apartment. While you do not earn a salary, your needs are met by the community: free housing, free meals in the dining hall, free education, free medical care. In your old age, you are cared for in the kibbutz until you die. Also, you receive a vacation once every seven to 10 years, depending on the resources of the kibbutz, which will pay for your trip overseas.

In the early years of Jewish immigration, mostly from Europe, the idea behind the kibbutz was to organize a society where everyone shared and contributed equally to the success of the community. Children lived in children's homes, each age cared for by a woman assigned to that home, freeing the remaining mothers to work full time. Labor was at a premium in the fields. The kibbutzim were a small (about 3% of the population) but vital part of Israeli society. Today, they have virtually disappeared as the young people no longer wish to live without money and most of them have converted to normal small towns.

My kibbutz, of about 1,000 people, had 400 head of cattle, orange, lemon and avocado groves, and, together with another kibbutz across the highway, staffed a frozen juice factory that sold mostly to Europe and, at the time, I was told, grossed about $40 million a year. It was a prosperous kibbutz. At the end of each year, a commission of the members decided how to spend the previous year's profits. For example, a new TV or telephone for each home, new cars for the kibbutz fleet or even another bedroom added to each home.

Ironically, the original idea of freeing women from being stay-at-home mothers had been subverted over time. The women on our kibbutz were channeled into more "traditional" women's roles, working in the laundry, dining hall and children's homes.

Geshom Hapoel, like all the sports clubs in Israel, was directly affiliated with one of the political parties, in our case, the Labor Party. Funding for the club came from the political party and, in return, the party (Hapoel) reaped the publicity when the club did well. My salary came from the party but the kibbutz contributed my housing and food. I had an enthusiastic manager, Gershon Shefa, the former coach of the club, who was able to twist arms and get the support of the kibbutz for this arrangement. They also paid my plane fare from the US.

There were those traditionalists on the kibbutz who were not happy with my presence because I was earning a salary. Gershon asked me to appease them by working voluntarily in the kitchen, scrubbing pots and pans once a month, which I did. In addition to the Israelis, there were also several dozen or more—depending on the time of year—young foreign volunteer workers who spent anywhere from two to six months as serfs, shoveling shit in the cow shed or picking oranges in the fields and, more often than not, getting drunk in the evenings. They received free housing and food, cigarette money and a couple of tours around Israel. Virtually all the volunteers were from Europe and the US.

My swim team was actually a regional team, pulling in swimmers from several towns and kibbutzim in the area. I had some better-than-average swimmers. Most of the older boys were in the army but in a special program that allowed them to train on a daily basis and generally do lighter duties during the day. There were always snafus, though. When

Israel sent in soldiers to the Sinai to remove the hard line settlers who refused to return the Sinai to Egypt, my swimmers were called up and it took us two weeks to get them back. Before the 1982 World Championships, they disappeared for a month during the invasion of Lebanon. The brother of one of my swimmers, a water polo player, was killed by a sniper during that war.

We had an old 25 meter pool to train in at Givat Haim, with a canvas bubble for the chilly winter months. The bubble was maintained by an air blower. When blackouts occurred, we had about three minutes to vacate the pool before the bubble collapsed completely. The back-up generator didn't always work, either. That first winter in Israel, I was upset to find that each month when I went to get my paycheck, the amount had been reduced and no explanations were given. In the kibbutz, I was moved around like a chess piece, forced to change apartments on five occasions during the five months I spent there that first winter. Totally disillusioned with the way I was treated and the other side of Israel that I was exposed to as a resident, as opposed to the red carpet treatment I got as a tourist, I decided to leave after the winter short course championships at the end of February.

When I mention the other side, I am referring to the arrogance of the Israelis who treat foreigners and even non-Israeli Jews with disdain. Rudeness is a practiced art in Israel. The other thing that bothered me was the tremendous influence of the Orthodox Jews on Israeli society, even though they only make up about 15% of the population. Since the creation of Israel, neither of the two major political parties has ever won an election outright. Following elections, a ruling coalition is formed.

The radical religious parties sell their votes dearly, receiving ridiculous concessions from one or the other of the major parties, such as: all restaurants in Israel must be kosher, pork is not officially served, though you could find a few that would serve "that other white meat." At the time, movies could not be shown on the Sabbath, nor was public transportation available; daylight savings time was not adopted because it would interfere with the morning prayers; El Al airlines couldn't fly on the Sabbath, and on and on.

When I flew to Israel, the rude Orthodox Jews would stand in the aisles of the plane swaying back and forth during their prayers in the morning and not allow the flight attendants to serve breakfast to the other passengers. In 1985, when I returned to Israel with my Greek team, we went to a meet in a West Bank town near Jerusalem on a Saturday, the Sabbath. From a distance, I saw what looked to be a mass of black ants. As we arrived, they turned out to be the Hassidic Jews in their black robes protesting that the pool would be open on Saturdays. As my Greek swimmers, ages 11-15, arrived, these holier-than -thou Jews spit on my girls because they were females and not covered from wrist to ankle. Soldiers had to shove them back to open a corridor for the swimmers to pass.

At the short course championships that winter, we had a fantastic meet, winning by a 2:1 score over the second place team, breaking several national records and impressing the politicians. I was called by the Hapoel people and asked to remain in Israel. They agreed to pay the portion of my salary that had been cut each month, offered me a new contract and said I would be the 1984 Israeli Olympic coach if I remained. I had already made plans to travel around the Mediterranean for the next six months but agreed to return that fall for another two years.

When I went back to Chicago that summer to visit my Mom, I even went to the Israeli consulate in Chicago and convinced a rabbi that I was Jewish. That way they paid my transportation to Israel as an immigrant and shipped my personal effects for free.

Back in Israel in October 1982, I was very excited about the upcoming season culminating in the Hapoel Games in March, the talented group of swimmers I had, and the longer term goal of the Olympics. It didn't take more than a month for reality to burst my bubble. Once again, my salary was reduced every month and I was soon informed that another coach had been selected for the Olympic team. When I called the politicians who had convinced me to return, they never answered my calls.

The Kibbutz was a great place to jog; there was virtually no traffic on the roads. We had a nice 400 meter track, as well. One day, as I was running around the kibbutz past the entrance gate, a young woman with a backpack called to me and asked where the volunteers signed in. As I proceeded to give her directions I noticed that she was staring at me with a strange look on her face. I continued my run but later, at the dining hall for dinner, one of the volunteers called to me, "Hey, have you talked to the new Brazilian girl?"

I asked him to point her out and, sure enough, it was the young lady I had met earlier that day. I introduced myself in Portuguese and asked her where she was from. Sao Paulo, she responded. I told her that I had coached swimming at the Hebraica Club in Sao Paulo and she said she was a scholarship volleyball player there and had even dated one of my swimmers. Her name was Marisa.

I noticed she looked like she was in pain and asked if anything was wrong. She said that after she registered as a volunteer and signed the insurance papers, she had gone to the dorm and blacked out, hitting her chin on a metal table as she fell and breaking six teeth. The kibbutz, which had a medical dispensary, refused to even give her pain killers and said dental problems were not covered under her insurance policy, requiring her to take a cab to the nearest hospital in a neighboring town.

I was really upset by this treatment, typical of the Israelis, and asked her to get her insurance papers. As I began reading the paper, my gaze drifted down to her full signature and last name, Rotenberg. I looked up and asked, "Do you know Saulo Rotenberg?"

She put her head down and whispered, "He is my father."

"Son of a bitch," I yelled. He was the sports director who had fired me five years before. I calmed down and apologized. She had recognized me when she arrived that afternoon but was too scared of my possible reaction to tell me who she was.

I took her insurance form, which clearly stated all injuries were covered, to a lawyer I knew in Tel Aviv to examine it and see if her injury was covered under the policy. After a week, my friend called and said he could no longer get involved. He said pressure was put on him but wouldn't say from where. In the meantime, Marisa and I became lovers, but after sex all I could think of was, "If you could only see me now, Saulo."

Marisa was actually sent to Israel as a punishment by her father after he found marijuana in her drawer. It cost Marisa $3,500 to get her teeth fixed. The kibbutz didn't pay a penny of it.

Now the months dragged on. The previous summer on my trip around the Mediterranean, I had given two clinics at a club in the beautiful town of Hania, on the northwest coast of Crete. The club had asked if I was interested in working there full time but I told them of my commitment in Israel. When the Israeli experience turned sour again, I decided to write them and was pleased to find that the invitation was still standing. I planned to finish out the winter season in Israel and depart after the Hapoel Games in late April.

Life on the kibbutz was pretty boring. There was a coffee house where the volunteers would hang out evenings and I often drifted over for a game of chess. Sometimes, I would go into Tel Aviv for a movie but mostly stayed occupied with coaching and chasing women. Each week, the kibbutz would show a movie in the auditorium. It was usually some Disney-type family movie. I met an Israeli woman one day in the dining hall and she invited herself over to my apartment one evening. She offered to come over on movie night each week while her husband watched the baby at home. So, when the lights dimmed, she would sneak out and sneak back in before the lights came on again. It sure beat Disney!

I met a South African volunteer at a party and we went to my place after and then again for the next few nights until I had to leave for a three-day swim meet. When I returned, I went over to her apartment. She had a downcast look when I walked in and she said, "We need to talk."

We took a stroll and she confessed that she had slept with another guy the previous evening. I felt like a knife had stabbed my heart. I told her what I was feeling and how weird it was because we had just been having fun, with no emotional involvement. The feeling lasted about 15 minutes and I really relished every moment because I had never felt jealousy before (and never have again). I finally understood why morons go out and kill someone because of that nasty emotional reaction.

I even tried to learn Hebrew on that second stint in Israel, enrolling in a class for the volunteers. Rick Parker, son of the actress Eleanor Parker, was on the kibbutz that winter to learn Hebrew so he could get the supplementary raise TWA gave to the flight attendants who learned a second language. Rick and I hung out and tried to get the other volunteers to take the class seriously but the instructor was so pitiful, the students left her in tears on a daily basis. Tired of ducking wet tea bags and paper airplanes, Rick and I quit the class and ended up playing cards during class time. Neither of us learned Hebrew. My swimmers spoke anywhere from decent to excellent English, and the fact that I was counting my days in Israel reduced my motivation to learn.

As the Hapoel Games approached, the winter nationals were to be the tryouts. At the last minute, the Israeli Federation, at the request of some of the coaches, announced that they would not score points that year. I was livid. It was an attempt by the other coaches to deny us another victory. After the tryouts, I had the most swimmers on the national team. The federation would choose four coaches for the national team but the Israeli coaches decided I was not to be one of them. My swimmers protested to the president of the federation. The next day he asked to talk to me, mentioning that he had seen an article of mine published in Swimming Technique magazine, about the injustices I had been witness to during my years coaching in South America.

The light bulb flashed in my head and I said that I was working on an article about my Israeli experience, too. The next day, I was notified that I would be one of the national coaches. The Israelis do not like criticism, especially published in the US, their big benefactor. Unlike the Maccabiah Games, which were limited to Jewish athletes from around the world, the Hapoel Games, also held every four years in Israel, were for any athletes from western, non-communist countries. At the Games, my swimmers performed very well, bagging two gold medals, swimming against the US, Germany, and others. It was my swan song.

Two days later, armed with two cheesecakes and a bottle of Kahlua, I boarded a boat in Haifa for the two-day cruise to Crete.

Chapter IX
Crete, Greece, 1983-87

Arriving in Heraklion, the main port of Crete, I was pleased to see a large contingent of the Hania swimmers there to greet me. The previous summer during the clinics there, I had asked one of the older girls who spoke very good English to help translate for the younger kids. One day, I saw that Soula hadn't put on her suit and it was just about time to begin the session. I asked her if she was getting in the water. She said she was sick. I didn't think much of it, though, the next day, when I saw her running around the deck but not in her swimsuit I suspected what it was.

"Soula, are you getting in today?"

"No," she replied, "I'm still sick."

I asked her if she was having her period and she said yes. So, I asked, "Why don't you swim? Women do all over the world."

She said that the doctors there told them that if they swam during their periods, they wouldn't be able to have children and, during her mother's time they didn't even bathe during those days! I wasn't going to worry about it since I was there for only another couple of days but when I decided to return and work there, I knew it would be an issue.

By the end of the first month, all the older girls had missed several days of practice. I asked Soula, who was no longer swimming, to call all the girls for a meeting and translate for me. I asked if they used tampons. One of the girls said no because it would take away their virginity. I put that myth to rest, left the room and Soula showed the girls how to insert a tampon. Before the moms knew what was happening, all the girls were using them and not missing practice. There were some ruffled feathers but it was a learning experience and the kids were improving so fast that it was quickly forgotten.

At the end of the summer season, the club asked me to remain. I already had plans for my first trip to Asia, organized by one of the SIU swimmers, Ral Rosario, a Filipino who swam in the US during his high school and college years and was now back in Manila, but agreed to return to Hania in January.

On the Asian trip, Ral, Asian Champion in the 200 free in 1978 and still the most famous swimmer the Philippines has produced, set up clinics for me in the Philippines, Indonesia, Singapore, Malaysia and Thailand. What a great trip it was. The Asian kids are so respectful, which made the clinics fun. It is truly a pleasure to work with them. In addition to the clinics, I had the opportunity to visit many of the tourist spots. It really whetted my appetite for that region of the world and I have returned many times, eventually visiting almost all of the countries in Asia.

In Hania, I located a nice apartment, part of an old Venetian house 50 meters from the beach, with a balcony that looked towards the water in one direction and the snow-capped mountains in the other. I was living the dream.

We had a thousand kids in our summer lesson program and it wasn't long before people began recognizing the American coach on the street, in restaurants and shops. Everyone was so friendly. I took the swimmers to Germany and Israel on swimming trips and to other Greek cities on training trips over the Easter week holiday. Crete was also a nice place to meet tourists. One afternoon, I saw a Chinese couple looking lost and gazing at their map in downtown Hania. I went over, gave them directions and invited them to lunch. We exchanged addresses and a year later, I called them up from Bangkok and was invited to spend a week with them in Hong Kong, another wonderful experience.

One summer day, I took my towel and went down to my beach. Noticing a stunning blonde sunning herself, I put my towel down nearby and started a conversation. It turned out Kiki was Dutch and had lived with her family just down the road several years before when her father was stationed at the NATO missile base just outside town. I invited her for dinner that night but she said she would have to ask her parents.

Kiki took off her large sunglasses and I asked, "Wait a minute, how old are you?"

When she said she was 16, I apologized and said forget about dinner. She answered, "Let's just see what my mom says."

Just that moment, her mom, dad and little brother came strolling back along the beach. She went to her mom and I could see the dagger looks being directed towards me. But, lo and behold, she came back with permission. Well, we had dinner, exchanged addresses and sent the occasional postcard over the next year and a half.

One day, around Christmas, I entered the swimming club office and the secretary said, "Hey Rick, call this number. Some woman wants to talk to you."

I called the local number and it was Kiki's mom who was back in Hania visiting old friends. She asked if we could meet for coffee. So, we met at a bar and she was very unfriendly but said she had promised her daughter to say hello to me while there. Then she mentioned that she had just been divorced and if I ever traveled to Holland, I was welcome to stop by. I took her phone number, thanked her and left, never expecting to see her again. But, what did I know about predicting the future.

The next summer, on my way to visit a German woman I had met in Hania, I called to get directions to her house and she said that I shouldn't come because she had a new boyfriend. What next? I looked through my address book and decided to give Kiki a call. Her mom answered and I asked if her offer was still open. She said yes, told me to take a train from Germany and that Kiki would meet me at the station in Arnhem. When I arrived, this incredibly beautiful woman came and gave me a huge, warm hug. You can probably guess what was going through my mind. We went to a nearby restaurant where Kiki worked as a waitress and she asked if I could wait about an hour for her to finish work. She would stop by my table whenever she could. At one point, a handsome young guy walked up to her and kissed her. She brought him over and introduced him as her boyfriend. My heart dropped but, oh well, it was too good to be true, anyway.

After work, we went for a drive, had dinner and she said they would drop me off at her mom's apartment for the night and pick me up the next morning. Her mom was in Germany with her boyfriend that weekend. Okay, no problem. I took a shower and was just about to crawl into bed when someone tried to open the front door. I had the chain on and asked who was there. It was Kiki's mom. I unlatched it and she came in.

"You're not planning on sleeping already, are you? Let's smoke a joint and have a drink," she said. Before I knew what hit me, we were in bed. "Just don't tell Kiki," she said. "She thinks I'm with my boyfriend." After a couple of hours of great sex, she sat me up and gave me the compliment of a lifetime, "I just wish you had been the first to sleep with my daughter."

It doesn't get any better than that. Kiki and her boyfriend came to visit me the next summer in Greece. Her mom married the German boyfriend.

It was also in Greece that I got a wake up call. In my water bed with a recent American college graduate who was heading for grad school at the University of Chicago, the young lady looked at me and said, "I just thought of something. You are older than my father." We had met on the ferry coming across from Athens. I guess she wasn't too disturbed by her realization because we hooked up again in Chicago a month later.

Lifting weights one day in the gym at the club, I was looking out the window and saw a nice blond walking along the sidewalk. I yelled out to her and she came in. We chatted for a while. She was from San Francisco where she worked in a dance studio. My club had a large vacant room that had been rented to a series of unsuccessful restaurants over the years so, the idea of using it as a dance/aerobic studio occurred to me. I asked her if she was interested and she agreed to return the following week from Heraklion, another city on Crete, where she was living with a boyfriend, for an interview with the club president who agreed that it seemed like a good idea for the club. I asked her to bring her résumé.

The following week, she showed up on time and we went up to the president's office. I asked her for her résumé but to our astonishment, she kicked her leg up into the air and said, "This is my résumé." I shrugged my shoulders and apologized to the president as I ushered her out of the office.

I said, "I don't know what you were thinking but that doesn't cut it."

Anyway, I had promised that she could stay at my place for the weekend, with ulterior motives of course, but was by that time totally turned off. We had dinner and took a cab to my house. It was late and I said I had to get some sleep because I had practice early the next morning, Saturday. I lay in my water bed and she was on another bed in the same room. It seemed like minutes after I fell asleep that the light went on. I looked over at her bed and she was sitting up devouring a huge salami sandwich, crumbs falling like snow on the sheets.

I said, "I thought you were a vegetarian? At least turn off the light."

I fell asleep to the sound of crunching. Shortly after, the light was on again and there she was eating another foot-long salami sandwich. I couldn't get back to sleep and when dawn came, I told her to get her things together and I would drop her off at a hotel in town before going to the pool. She wasn't happy about that.

About 15 minutes after practice started, who did I see walking towards the pool from town? She stormed into the pool and in front of all the parents in the stands screamed, "You motherfucker, how dare you do that to me." I quietly walked over and in a calm voice told her to get off the deck before I called the police. It worked and I never saw her again. Win some, lose some.

One big problem I had to resolve living in Greece, was how to change my Greek currency to US dollars so I could bring my earnings back to the US each year. It was illegal to buy US dollars at that time, unless you were a legal resident, which I wasn't, and could prove you were going on a trip out of the country. So, each month I would get in a line at one or more of the local banks where tourists were waiting to exchange their foreign currency and whisper in someone's ear that I wanted to buy their dollars and would pay a better rate. Most people would then quietly follow me out of the bank and we would do our transaction where we couldn't be seen. I then stored my accumulated dollars under my water bed until my annual trip home at the end of August.

It was all quite risky but my choices were limited. One summer, I was about to leave Athens on my way to a stopover in Venice, waiting in the port for my boat to arrive when two harbor police walked by, turned to me and asked in English how many dollars I had on me. I had about seven grand stashed in various places but admitted to two thousand. They told me to accompany them to an office where they asked to see my money. Fortunately, they weren't interested in Travelers Checks and didn't notice that mine were all from other persons. But when they saw my wad of $100 dollar bills, one said to the other in Greek, "It is counterfeit."

His partner was doubtful but they agreed to call a guy from a bank to come over and verify. I pretended that I didn't understand Greek and sat reading my pocket book. About a half hour later, a harried guy came running in, took a couple of the bills and after rubbing them on a clean sheet of paper, called the policemen assholes and said it was real money. One of the cops said to the other they should keep some anyway but the first said no, to return them.

I was lucky that day. In addition they hadn't checked my wallet which had several thousand more. When I returned to Greece each fall, I would have hundreds of swimming caps and goggles in my luggage to sell to the Greek swimmers. Each time I went through customs, I would act like the tourist idiot asking in a loud voice, "Where are the boats to the islands?" or "Where is a good hotel?" The customs officials always waved me through, saying to each other, another *malakas* (asshole) American.

The old port in Hania is a beautiful place with a classic lighthouse and ringed with restaurants and sidewalk cafés. One of the tourist town rituals plays out every summer night. The Greek guys, locals and soldiers stationed just outside of Hania, occupy the first row of seats at the cafés and check out the tourist women who strut their stuff walking back and forth along the harbor. The guys sing out in their accented English. "Hey, you are very beautiful, come and have a Nescafe with me." Enough of them are actually successful that they never give up.

A year before I went to Greece, my girlfriend at SIU took a vacation in Greece and spent a few days in Hania. She was exuberant when she returned, having met her Greek god at a bar in Hania, and spent passionate nights with him. The next year, when I found out that I would be visiting Hania, I wrote her and said I would say hi to her Greek god for her. She sent me his name and the location of the bar he owned. One evening, I located the bar and asked for Kostas. The guy I asked—a fat, unshaven, smelly sloth, said it was he. In total shock, I left quickly and pondered over it for the next few days. I guess that a few shots of *ouzo* can do strange things to a woman's perceptions.

In Hania, we had a nice swimming pool complex, a 50 meter salt water pool which was emptied and cleaned every week, a 25 meter fresh water pool, and a small teaching pool. Training in salt water isn't fun. The salt actually cakes on your skin and, if not for the gallon jar of Vaseline that the girls plastered on their skin where their suits rubbed, they would have been bleeding by the end of practice. It was a municipal pool and, unlike every other municipal pool in Greece, we shared it only with the water polo team.

At a similar complex in Iraklion, there were often as many as five or six teams, all fighting for lanes, as was the case in most pools in Greece. If a parent didn't like the coach of his team, he could form another team and demand a lane. It was absolute chaos, and a major reason why Greece was a swimming backwater in those days.

The regional president of the swimming association was a Mr. Zambiozis from one of the Iraklion clubs. Because the clubs there were much smaller, he would arbitrarily rule that only two swimmers were allowed to compete in each event per team. The purpose of this absurd rule was to limit my much larger team's chances of winning. An even worse result was that some of my swimmers never got an opportunity to compete because we often had six to eight swimmers prepared to swim each event. My protests, as usual, fell on deaf ears. After one shouting match, Zambiozis proclaimed that he would be in power for "another 100 years."

By Greek rules, once a swimmer won a medal (top three in any national age group championship), he was stuck for life with that team and could not transfer to another. The exception to the rule seemed to be a couple of the big soccer clubs in Athens who, mysteriously, were able to recruit swimmers from the smaller towns for their swim teams and acquire immediate eligibility for them. I lost two of my best swimmers this way. Eventually, they needed to leave Hania, anyway, because we didn't have a reputable university.

The Greek swimming federation is a bunch of good old boys who continue in power even today, 21 years after I left. They made decisions that were detrimental to the swimmers. I would send them suggestions that were routinely ignored. For example, when FINA (Federation Internationale de Natation, the world governing body for swimming) changed the breaststroke rule allowing the head to go underwater, the Federation rejected it and continued to disqualify swimmers for another six months. When I showed them the written FINA rule change, they said I didn't know how to read English.

In the last three years of my stay, I was called before a Sports Court each year where I was accused of disrespecting the Federation by going to the newspapers with my criticisms. With my translator, I would explain that I had gone first to the Federation but, being ignored, had no choice but to go to the media. I explained why I criticized the decisions of the federation and was always exonerated.

In Crete, the regional swimming officials from Iraklion actually announced to the coaches at national qualifying meets that it was okay to false start so that the swimmers would have a better chance of making the qualifying times. At that time in Greece, before the no-false-start rule was adopted, swimmers regularly false started in almost every event at all competitions. I won't bore the reader with more examples of the irregularities I witnessed there but as I go over my notes from those years, I feel my blood pressure rising again.

Another source of conflict was the fact that coaches invariably smoked on deck while training their swimmers. I would ask them to stop but that would trigger some anti-American response.

There was a provincial championship that involved the teams of all the towns outside of Athens and Salonika. We won that meet three years in row. It was a source of pride for the team and our town.

After four years in Hania, I decided to move on. I loved the town and the people but the limiting factor was that when the swimmers got faster, they were recruited by the Athens clubs and moved on or went away to school in a larger city. The horrible winter of 1986, when it snowed three times, rained for most of four months and waves from the Mediterranean washed over the 14-foot wall into the pool, nailed that coffin.

My best swimmer, Tonia Mahaira, who was the top Greek female sprinter for many years and made two Olympic teams, stuck with me. When I left in 1987, I sent her to Clovis, CA for her senior year of high school and then got her a scholarship to SIU. She eventually earned a Masters in Nutrition at St. Louis University, returned to Greece and continued swimming while working as a nutritionist. Outspoken and always a thorn in the side of the politicians who ran the federation, she continued to defy the odds and remained one of the top Greek swimmers until the summer of 2004 when she was 33 year old.

Ten days before the Athens Olympics for which Tonia had already qualified, the Federation notified all the newspapers that she had failed a drug test the previous day and was kicked off the team. The drug test results had not even been released. When they did come out, her test was negative but it was too late for the Olympics. It was a devastating event in her life. She sued the federation and the newspapers and three years later, won a settlement of a quarter of a million Euros. The scumbags who did this are still running the federation.

Tonia remains one of my best friends. Whenever possible, I go back to Hania to celebrate Greek Easter and the traditional skewered goat at her parents' house. In 2003 and 2007, I took my US masters team to Hania for a swim meet and the opportunity to enjoy the beauty of the Greek Islands.

Chapter X
Malaysia, 1988

Leaving Hania at the end of the summer in 1987, I traveled for several months. I had stayed in touch with one of the swimmers I worked with during clinics in Malaysia and through her dad, the President of the Swimming Federation, I received an offer to prepare the Malaysian team for the Asian Swimming Championships to be held in Guangzhou, China in late April, 1988. I spent four months in Kuala Lumpur, the capital of Malaysia.

Malaysia has an interesting history. Millions of Chinese had immigrated to Malaysia and during the British colonial period dominated the economy of the country despite the fact that they comprised a minority of the population. Following independence, the Malay majority passed what are called the Bumiputra laws which, basically, give the majority Malays many advantages to "catch up" with the Chinese. For example, after the entrance exam results for the universities are released each year, it is obvious from the names of the students, that almost all the top students are Chinese but the Malays are given first choice to enter the universities and many of the Chinese are forced to go overseas to get their college education. Cheap government loans are offered to Malays to start businesses, but not to the Chinese.

When the Malaysian team was chosen, all the swimmers who qualified were Chinese. Generally, the Malays don't go into competitive swimming. But, in order to get any funding from the government for the trip to China, we had to take a Malay girl whose father was an influential banker, even though the girl had not achieved a qualifying time. The Malay girl's older sister, a university student, often picked her up after practice in a gleaming white Mercedes.

One day, the sister asked me how I was doing. I said that it was a little boring in KL. She offered to take me around to see the city and the next day we went to the National Museum, at the time a very beautiful building, but mostly empty inside. When she asked if there was any place else I would like to visit, her tone and eyes conveyed the message that opened the door. I said we could go to my hotel and listen to some music on my tape player. Arriving at the hotel, we couldn't risk going up together, so I sent her up first in one elevator while I entered from the back and took another elevator. We timed it just right, reaching my door simultaneously.

As I locked the door behind us, the phone rang. I thought, "Busted," but it was only a phone call for me. The guy on the line was the father of a couple of young swimmers who had participated in one of my clinics and wanted me to give them extra lessons. I told him I really didn't have the time but he said, "Let's chat about it." And then he announced that he was in the lobby of the hotel and would come right up.

I said, no, I wasn't feeling well but he said it was important and hung up. I told the girl that this guy was coming up and she asked who it was. It turned out he was a close friend of her father! In panic, she hid in the bathtub. When he came up, I wouldn't let him in, pleading an upset stomach and he finally went away. Close call. I continued meeting the Malay girl until she began to get overconfident, wanting to hold hands in public. Since I had no intention of leaving Malaysia in a casket, I finally broke it off.

Tina Turner was on a world tour that fall and winter of 1987-88. I was able to get tickets while in Brazil in December and enjoyed her concert before 60,000 fans at a soccer stadium in Sao Paulo. To my delight, she came to Malaysia on that same tour. I talked my swim team into attending her concert in the capital, Kuala Lumpur. The venue was an indoor basketball gym that seated only around 5,000. When Tina began her first number, the young people in the front rows, mostly students at the International School, immediately stood up and began to dance.

Suddenly, the sound went off and a police officer jumped up on stage, grabbing the microphone away from Tina. He announced that everyone must remain seated or the concert would be cancelled. Tina protested but to no avail. Can you imagine sitting quietly through a Tina Turner concert?

The trip to Guangzou from Malaysia for the Asian Swimming Championships was an odyssey in itself. Flying first to Hong Kong, some of our luggage was missing but fortunately was located after an hour, before being sent to Canada instead of Canton(the English name of Guangzhou). We had a bus waiting to drive us to Guangzhou but were then informed that it was only going to drop us at the railway station where we would ride a train to the border. There was a line of people waiting for that train that snaked around the building twice. It was a holiday weekend and it looked like everyone wanted to go to the mainland. We finally squeezed onto the train. When it arrived at the border, everyone had to go through customs. As the doors of the train opened, people ran at full speed to the customs booths. The police climbed up on the fences to avoid getting trampled.

I lost all of my swimmers in the crowd. One of the coaches had his wallet lifted. We regrouped on the Chinese side of the border and tried to find our next bus to continue the journey. We walked for blocks in the rain until we connected with our bus. By then, it was night. The headlights on the bus failed several times and the driver would put his head under the hood and light a match to check the connections. Every time he did that, I had the kids leave the bus for fear it would catch fire. In Guangzhou, the driver got lost and it took another hour to find our hotel. We arrived well past midnight.

The next day, the visiting teams' delegates and coaches had a meeting with the host Chinese swimming officials. The Chinese delegate who chaired the meeting suggested that we were all friends and there was no need to do any drug testing. Amazingly, everyone agreed. At the meet, a Chinese swimmer broke a world record in the 50 free, beginning a long period of record breaking that culminated in the Asian Games in 1994 in Hiroshima when a dozen Chinese athletes tested positive for illegal drugs and were disqualified.

The traditional Chinese breakfast is high in fat content. Therefore I had the Malaysian swimmers bring plenty of cereal for a low fat breakfast. The Chinese manager of the hotel asked what each country's nutritional needs were so I said we would like cold milk in the morning for our cereal. The first morning, the waitress brought us boiling milk. When I told her we needed cold milk, she brought us a large bowl of ice to cool the milk. The next morning, she brought us quarts of frozen milk and later, boiling water to melt the ice milk. One day, we toured the central market, taking pictures of the cute dogs, cats, monkeys and even snakes, all waiting to be killed, skinned and cooked.

Our top swimmer at the meet, Nural, was a young lady who was the granddaughter of the President of Singapore. She attended school and trained in Australia and, though Malaysian Chinese, her politically astute mom had changed her name to a Malay/Muslim name so that she could get funding from the Malaysian government. The mom was unbearable, a snob who thought she could do as she pleased and antagonized everyone in the delegation. I really felt sorry for the daughter who was manipulated by her mother.

Nural was one of the favorites in the 200 free. When the official whistled the swimmers to the blocks, Nural was still rinsing her goggles at the diving pool. As the other swimmers got up on the blocks, she was still strolling in the direction of the blocks. When the starter said, "Take your marks," she realized that she was in trouble and ran to the blocks while putting on her goggles. She took a running start, entering after all the other swimmers, and still managed a 3rd place finish. Her mom ran down on deck and tried to have the results annulled and the race swum again. The Chinese, of course, ignored her. To them she was no one special. It was a hard lesson for Nural but, I hope, a learning experience.

At the post-meet banquet for all the participants, we sat at large round tables that seated about a dozen people each. There was plenty of Chinese rice wine and the bottles were replaced as quickly as they were emptied. At my table were most of the swimmers, including our best distance swimmer, 16-year old Jeffrey Ong. Jeffrey's dad was Malaysian Chinese and his mother was British. Though he was over six feet tall his mother treated him like a baby, cutting his meat for him into bite size pieces at the table. Jeffrey never complained but everyone else was embarrassed for him. At one point during the banquet, his mom, who was seated directly across from him, said, in a stern voice "Jeffrey, I think you've had enough to drink."

Jeffrey, bleary eyed, pointed at her and replied, "You're not my mother now." People at the table actually applauded. His mom didn't say another word.

During the meet, I introduced myself to as many Chinese coaches as possible and told them that I would be traveling in China for two weeks after the meet. The Chinese asked for my travel plans and notified local sports authorities to look after me. My first stop was Xian, the ancient walled city where the famous terra cotta soldiers were discovered. My flight was delayed for six hours. I was the only westerner on the plane. When we landed at 2:30 AM at an airport with no lights on and a mass of people waiting in the dark behind barriers for the passengers to deplane, I admit, I was a bit nervous. Miraculously, as I followed the other passengers toward a dark building up ahead, a voice in the crowd shouted out, "Rick Powers!"

What a relief. It was a PE professor from the local sports institute who had recently returned from a year at UCLA. He took me to the hotel but the gate was locked and the guard not to be found. Next, we went to a hostel for students. There were no vacancies, so he rousted the guard out of his bed and gave it to me for the remainder of the night. At 6 AM, he came back for me and we were finally able to get into the hotel. He asked me where I wanted to go and took me to a provincial swimming school where the best area swimmers lived and trained. The driver from the sports institute, who didn't speak a word of English, was then assigned to drive me to all the tourist sites for the next two days. That culminated in a banquet at his tiny house with all the neighbors leaning in on the window sills to watch the American chow down. It was my best meal in China, although I can only guess what I was eating. There were no stray dogs or cats in the streets.

I planned to spend the following week in Beijing attending the workouts of the Chinese national team and visiting the Forbidden City, the Great Wall and other fascinating sites, but I was unable to book a flight. The computer system wasn't working. The guy from UCLA, took me to the train station where his cousin worked and was able to get me a ticket for a "hard sleeper." This was a sleeping car with slabs of wood to sleep on and no sheets or pillows. I arranged my clothing on the wood to provide some comfort. The compartments on the train were open, with no sliding doors to cut the noise. All night long I suffered through the sounds of the Chinese hacking and spitting, yes, on the floor. In the morning, I went to the bathroom to pee and brush my teeth. I slid down the corridor on the spit and when I reached the basin to brush, it was covered with shit. At that time, diapers were a luxury so infants clothing just had a slit on the ass allowing them to shit wherever, meaning the sink on trains. People were very friendly, shared their snacks and tried their two or three words of English on me. Twenty two hours later, I arrived in Beijing.

One night, I had dinner at the apartment of the Chinese national team head coach. He and his wife, one of China's leading eye specialists, each made about $40 a month. The cab drivers, who got tips in foreign currency and scammed the tourists, made five times that. The next year, I helped the Chinese coach find a spot in the US, where he has remained.

Back in Malaysia, I was asked to do a clinic in one of the outlying states. When I arrived at the pool for an orientation session on the first day, there were about 50 people waiting in the stands: coaches, swimmers and parents. Later, back at my hotel, I was watching the news on TV when the telephone rang. The woman on the line said she had attended that first session and would like to ask me a question. I said, sure, go ahead, and she began to tell me about her daughter's coach who was mean and who always punished her, but I cut in and made it clear that I wasn't there to get involved in local politics.

But, she said, "He makes her do frog jumps almost every day." Again, I said, well, I don't even know what frog jumps are and I really don't want to get into that. She asked if I would be at the hotel for a while and then hung up. About 20 minutes later, there was a knock on my door. There she was. We ended up doing a modified version of the frog jumps for the next couple of hours. Her husband was traveling overseas. Right place, right time.

The next day, I was at the pool with the guy assigned to accompany me by the state government. As I prepared to enter the water to demonstrate a drill, someone from the front gate came running towards me screaming in Malay. My guide started to argue with him and he finally went away but giving me the evil eye all the time. I asked the guide what that was all about. "Well, he saw you putting your goggles on and males are not allowed to wear goggles in this state because everyone knows they just use them to look at the women under water. But he relented and will make an exception for you."

The next day, on the way to the pool for the morning session, my guide, a heavy, beer-bellied smoker, asked me, "Are you a free thinker?" Not having a clue what he was referring to, I sort of hemmed and hawed. He said he knew there were a lot of Aussies and Germans who were freethinkers and would I like to fuck his wife! Not one to commit, sight unseen, I gave a non-committal answer. After lunch, he arrived at the hotel. When he knocked, I was just getting out of the shower. I opened the door and he came in and sat down while I dressed, showing more than the average interest as I took the towel off. I thought, uh oh, he wants to bonk me while I'm doing his wife. Now how do I get out of this?

That evening on the way to the hotel, we picked up his wife, a lovely, petite Chinese woman. After dinner he said, "Take my wife to your room. I'll get a bottle of scotch from the car and be right up." As soon as we entered the room, I asked his wife if this was something she had a choice in. She said no. When my guide arrived, I nixed the plan and he didn't get upset at all. Anyway, I still had plenty of frog jumps to keep me out of trouble.

For Malay New Year, my guide told me we would visit the home of one of his workers and to prepare for a feast. I was on my third plate of food when he said, "What do you think you are doing? We still have seven more homes to visit." I have never been so stuffed. As we walked into the last house, I looked at all the photos of race horses on the walls and joked to my guide that we would probably chow down on the horse that lost. Sure enough, it was horse meat we were served.

On a previous trip to Malaysia, following a clinic in Kuala Lumpur, I was invited by one of the coaches to go to a town in the north. Malaysia is one of the world's leading producers of tin, palm oil and rubber. One of that coach's friends who owned a tin mine invited me to visit his mine. On the highway, headed towards the mine, I saw a large factory being assembled and asked my host what it was for. "Oh, that is an asbestos plant that was shut down in the US. We bought it cheap." He shocked me further when he said the asbestos was to be used to line the water pipes of the city. It's definitely a place where you might want to drink bottled water.

We toured his open pit mine and saw the ore being refined by sluicing, then further refined in a building where it was handled by women with no protective gear. I didn't think anything of it until we passed an open shed filled with barrels labeled "Danger: Radioactive Material." Curious, I asked the owner what they were doing there. He replied that one of the by-products of the tin refinement was this radioactive material that was sold and shipped to Japan.

I said, "But those women refining the ore have no protection."

He replied that it wasn't THAT radioactive. A week later, the front page of a newspaper in Kuala Lumpur had an article about women working in the tin mines who were dying of cancer.

Chapter XI
Perks

There are a few perks being an American coach overseas. In most of the Latin American countries at that time, the macho males dominated their societies. It was a rare male who didn't go to prostitutes or have lovers on the side. When a US senator was caught with a prostitute and resigned, there was a joke in one of the Brazilian newspapers which said that if that were the criteria, there would be no one left to govern Brazil. Often, marriage was for a good business or social connection and, especially among much of the upper class, the wife was expected to look pretty, take care of the house and the maids, and be an exemplary hostess at parties and dinners. While the husbands were out roaming, their spouses were expected to be good little wives.

The men bragged about their sexual conquests; the women had to be very discreet about their own affairs. The wives often dropped the kids off at the pool and picked them up after practice. Aware of the rapport I had with their children, they often felt that I could be trusted. The fathers of my swimmers sometimes asked if they could use my apartment for their trysts but I always refused. I clearly remember one father telling me that he makes babies with his wife but when he wants to have "good" sex, he goes to a prostitute with whom he can play out his fantasies.

Understandably, young Brazilian boys had a skewed idea of what a woman was all about. It was very common for the boys, often shortly after puberty, to receive money to spend at a brothel from an uncle or grandfather.

Getting your sexual initiation from a prostitute at an early age sets the tone for a lack of respect for women in general, and fosters the impression that, sexually, women are just to be used. On one swimming trip in Brazil, my assistant Lula and I had a long conversation with several of our teenage boy swimmers, explaining to them how much better sex was with a woman you loved and respected as a human being, rather than just a sex object. The boys were attentive. They had obviously never had that perspective presented to them before.

On the other side, for many years, I would have a sex education talk with my older teenage girls. I covered topics as varied as getting an education so that you would never be dependent on a man and could fend for yourself in case your marriage didn't last; what actually happens to your body during your menstrual period; what turns both men and women on sexually; birth control, including abortion; and sex for physical enjoyment, not just procreation. I was always amazed at how ignorant the girls were about their bodies and how grateful they were to have the opportunity to talk openly about those topics. Over the years, many of them would tell me about their sexual experiences without the slightest embarrassment. I don't recall a single one who had ever had a similar conversation with their father.

One woman in Sao Paulo I got the nod from, came to my house one day and knocked on the door. She was wearing a mink coat and carrying a couple of bags of food purchased at the supermarket. She brought the bags with her so they wouldn't be stolen from her car. When she put the bags down and opened her coat, she was totally naked underneath. She had spent an hour shopping without a stitch on under her coat, just so she could surprise me.

On deck one day at the university pool in Caracas, in 1968, two lovely blondes walked in the gate. I went over and asked if I could be of help. They were the daughter and secretary of a visiting Swedish nuclear physicist. I invited the daughter to dinner. We ended up at my place and at about one AM, the father called, checking on her. I said we were on the way back. We dressed quickly and took a taxi to her hotel. After leaving her at her door, I went down to the waiting taxi. The driver was chatting with a police officer who asked for my ID card. As I reached for my wallet, I realized I had grabbed the wrong pair of pants. No ID. I was taken to jail for the remainder of the night and was only released the next morning. A lovely night ended so badly.

A week later, the professor left with his family but the secretary remained for another week. Though she was more than twice my age, she was nice and we went out a couple of times. While writing this paragraph, I remembered the daughter's name, did a search on Google and found her. She is now a professor at the University of Goteborg in Sweden.

At a national meet in Curitiba, Brazil, I ran into a woman I had known in Porto Alegre. She was the chaperone at the meet of my former team. We decided to go to one of the motels that you pay by the hour that evening after she put the team to bed. I asked a friend from Curitiba where the best place was. Approaching the motel in a taxi, we noticed that it was surrounded by police cars. I asked the taxi driver if he knew an alternative and he took us to another place. We left the city and drove a long ways through the dark countryside before seeing some lights in the distance. Driving up to the motel, I was dismayed to see a long line of cars waiting for vacant rooms. When our turn finally came, we took off our clothes and as we lay down on the bed, we were immediately attacked by hundreds of voracious mosquitoes so that we were unable to remain in the room. It was a miserable experience, and not cheap, what with the taxi drivers' exorbitant fee on top of the cost of the room.

When I began my second stint in Venezuela, one of the older swimmers who transferred to my team asked me one day if I was going to resume the affair I had during my previous stay, with another swimmer's mom. I asked him where he heard that and I denied it because it wasn't true. He just laughed, "Sure, Rick."

Soon after that, figuring that you can't win no matter what you do, I became involved with four of the mothers on the club. One day, when I was home in bed with one of them, the telephone rang and an irate voice asked, "How come Sheila is there with you?"

I replied, "How do you know that?" The woman who called was another one of the four. She had been called by her friend and told that she needed a ride to her lover's place, and it had to be a woman so that her husband wouldn't suspect anything. I actually don't remember how

I got out of that one. It was interesting to watch the dynamic in the stands at the pool when the mom's picked up their kids. By the end of my time there, everyone suspected everyone else and they wouldn't even say hi to each other. It was all pretty funny from my perspective down on deck.

At a dinner party in Sao Paulo, I was introduced to a beautiful woman by the mom of one of my swimmers. We ended up dating for quite some time. One day she said, "I think that one day you will sleep with Angela's daughter (my swimmer)."

I said, "You're out of your mind." But, sure enough, some years later, it happened. How do women know those things?

My assistant coach in Sao Paulo, Lula, introduced me to his sister. I asked her out and after dinner we went to her apartment. She lived with her brother. We were going at it on the living room floor when Lula walked in. I sort of froze, expecting my life to come to an abrupt end, but he just stepped over us and went to his room. The next day, I apologized but he said, "Don't worry about it. She's a big girl now."

I was in Singapore for a clinic in the early 80s when one of the swimming families invited me to dinner one evening. The father asked if I would like to tour the city the following day, his day off. We spent the day visiting a number of interesting sites and he bought me a pair of painted egg shells as a souvenir of my visit, which I have to this day. The next day, he died in an accident on the oil rig where he worked. Three years later, on another visit to the island nation, I went to the club and asked the coach about the kids of the guy who died in the accident during my previous visit. He said the club had allowed the wife to open a small noodle kiosk on the club grounds so she could support herself and the kids. He pointed it out and when I went over to say hello, putting out my hand to shake hers, she grasped my hand and wouldn't let go. Another one of those Kodak moments.

I asked if she would like to have dinner and, soon after, we were in bed at my hotel. She said that within her conservative community, she was still expected to behave like a widow and could not date. Once again, I just happened to be the right guy in the right place at the right time.

At SIU, I was having an affair with a very wealthy woman who would come over every Tuesday morning at 10 for a little stress relief. On the way out she would leave a $100 dollar bill. She knew I was hurting financially there and was just helping me out.

I was traveling in Morocco with a Norwegian guy for a couple of days. Sitting one afternoon at a café in the main plaza of Marrakesh, we struck up a conversation with a nice looking young lady who was sitting alone at the next table. Between the little bit of French that my friend knew and the few words of English that she knew, we were able to communicate and made plans for a date that evening. She would bring a friend and we would go dancing at a disco in one of the Western tourist hotels. All of a sudden, a guy on the other side of the café began to shout in Arabic and the young lady excused herself and quickly walked away. The guy ran up to our table and announced, "We don't allow our women to talk to foreigners."

But, apologetically, he offered to be our guide for the day to make up for what he had done. We thought, oh, another rip-off guide just trying to get our money. As it turned out, he was really nice and took us to great places. That night at 8:30, my friend and I returned to the café hoping the women would show up. They were waiting for us. We piled into a taxi, I in the back seat with the two women. As we pulled away from the curb, the women sank down almost to the floor. I asked why and they said so that no one should see them with foreigners. Soon, we arrived at the hotel. Walking up to the disco entrance, a passing Arab in his white robes grabbed one of the women and, shouting at her, began to drag her away.

I rushed over and grabbed him but the girl told me to get away because he had a knife. After a heated discussion of several minutes, he left her and we proceeded to the door of the disco. The guard at the door refused us entrance and said they didn't allow their women to come in with foreigners. That was the end of that attempt at intercultural communion. We dropped the girls off at the main square.

The next day, my friend began an attempt to cross North Africa by bicycle. He was never heard from again.

I took a train to Fez, my next stop. In the compartment, I struck up a conversation with a Moroccan woman in Western dress who, it turned out, was a journalist for a newspaper in Casablanca. I related the strange occurrences of the previous day and she told me that even after having lived in Europe for five years, her father would not allow her to date a foreigner. I asked what the local men do for sex since they have to marry a virgin bride. Her reply was astonishing, "They have sex among themselves, until they get married." Different strokes for different folks.

In another of Morocco's cities, Meknes, I walked for three hours in the hot sun to visit the royal granary, a large walled building on the outskirts of the city. As I walked up to the ticket window, I noticed several Mercedes Benzes with diplomatic plates parked in front.

The guy in the booth said, "Closed" and when I argued that it didn't close for two more hours, he finally just waved me in without collecting the entrance fee. I began walking through the dimly-lit stone corridors where the huge cisterns were. It was a gloomy place lit only by torches. As I went out to the gardens in back, the group of diplomats passed my on their way out. I heard a deep boom in the distance. After about half an hour, I returned to the front entrance, a door 20 feet high. It was locked, the guard nowhere to be found. I pounded on the door and yelled through a crack but the street was far away.

I knew no one would be back until the following day. The place looked like a set for "Raiders of the Lost Ark." I began to imagine the rats and bats coming out at night. Retracing my steps to the gardens in back, I found another huge door but this one had a narrow open space at the top. I collected some wooden crates I found and built a mound of debris high enough so that I could reach the top rim of the door. From there, I was able to pull myself up, slither through the opening and jump to the ground outside. For weeks I had nightmares about being trapped in that dungeon-like place.

In addition to the sexual perks, there are the health-related ones. Many of my former swimmers became doctors and dentists. For years after one of my swimmers, Jorge Pinto Ribeiro, from Porto Alegre became a cardiologist, I would receive a free checkup and EKG on each trip to that city. Jorge's brother, Sergio, also became a doctor and married another doctor. In 1987, while staying at Sergio's house I mentioned to him that I was thinking of having a vasectomy. He said that his wife, Carla, had just taken a class with a doctor who had recently returned from the US with all the latest updates on vasectomies. Carla called the doctor and made an appointment for that afternoon.

Doctors try to convince patients not to have the procedure, reasoning that they will want to have children some day. The vasectomy is reversible, though. After making it clear that I wanted the operation, the doctor asked me to choose the hospital. Sergio recommended one and the doctor said I needed to do a spermogram and blood test at that hospital and wrote out the request for the lab. Sergio and I drove over and I hurried up to the lab. When I walked in the door, I was surprised that it was empty except for a nurse behind the counter. I gave her the request and she gave me a plastic cup and said that the sample must be turned in within 15 minutes of ejaculation. I was too embarrassed to go in the rest room and beat off so I went down to Sergio's car and asked him if we could return in less than 15 minutes from his house. He said yes.

Returning home, I borrowed one of his wife's lotions, did the quickie and rushed back to the hospital. Reaching over the counter to hand the plastic cup to the nurse, she looked at me in surprise, "Oh, sir, I forgot to tell you we don't take samples after 4 PM." I sort of lost it and began a tirade about the incompetence so common in Brazil. She told me not to worry and gave me another plastic cup, telling me to come back the next morning. Of course, when I got into the car with the plastic cup, Sergio started laughing about how I must have really enjoyed the process.

The next morning, bright and early, I was in the bathroom working on another sample, when Carla knocked on the door asking if I needed any help. I yelled at her to leave me alone, that I was trying to focus. We took the trip, now in rush hour morning traffic, back to the lab. Arriving in 13 and a half minutes, all sweaty, I elbowed my way through the crowd to the counter, where some 10 nurses were lined up. A large ugly nurse came over and said, "Oh, no, who do you think you are? Take a number and sit down like everyone else."

I said, looking at my watch, "You have about 20 seconds to take this sample." Seeing what it was, she relented but told me to be seated and wait to be called for the blood sample.

About a half hour later, a doctor opened a door and called my name. He sat me in a small room and proceeded to lecture me on why I shouldn't have a vasectomy. I interrupted him and pointed out that I already had that conversation. Then, he pulled open a drawer and pulled out a plastic cup and asked me to get a sample for him! I asked what in the hell was going on here, relating the previous day's experience. He got indignant and asked me to point out the nurse that had forgotten to tell me about the 4 PM deadline.

I said that was history, but what about this morning's sample? Becoming more flustered, he promised to hunt it down while I waited. After about 15 minutes, I went out and asked a nurse where the doctor was. She had no idea but suggested we take the blood sample and I could return at 4 PM for the results. At 4, the sperm test results were still missing, with the operation scheduled that evening at 7 PM.

Back in the hospital at 7, the doc asked for the lab results. I proceeded to relate the various disasters of the previous 24 hours and between fits of laughter, he told me to stop while he went and called all the doctors and nurses he could find on the floor. I had to tell the story again, often drowned out by their laughter. One of the doctors said, "I told you guys this place was going to the dogs."

Finally, my doctor said to go change and not worry about the test results. A nurse put me on the gurney and wheeled me into the operating room. That wing of the hospital is old. The ceilings are very high. As I entered the operating room lying on my back, I noticed some red splotches on the ceiling. I said to the doctor, "Don't you think it might be nice to wipe the blood off the ceiling from time to time so the next patient feels a little more confident?"

He looked up and said, "That? Don't worry. It's from the last guy on whom I performed a vasectomy." I knew he was joking but...

So, now under the lights on the operating table, I was getting prepped when Sergio walked in and asked me if he could watch. "Sure," I answered. Then Carla walked in. "Well, why not, I wouldn't let you in the bathroom."

Soon, there were about 20 nurses and students gathered around. I was waiting for someone to wheel in a barbeque and a cooler of beer. Next, waiting for the local anesthetic to take effect, the doctor picked up his scalpel and waved it in my face, saying that he told me it would cost $100 dollars but he wanted $500. I said, "Whatever you want doc, just be careful what you cut with that scalpel."

When the operation began, Sergio yelled "Oh, no, he cut it off!"

I was so tense. At that point I failed to see the humor. But, all's well that ends well and, at least I know there aren't going to be any little Ricks running around the streets, so, it was worth the hassle and I got a good story out of it, too.

On another occasion, I broke the cap of a tooth for the fifth time and called my dentist in Davis, CA. He said recapping would cost over $900. I then called one of my former swimmers in Sao Paulo, Brazil, a dentist, and got a gold cap for only $300.

In 2002, I began to feel chest pains when I was running. My Kaiser Health plan doctor told me not to worry about it and, since the pain soon dissipated about 10 minutes into the run, I didn't take it too seriously. By early 2003, the discomfort I was feeling had extended to resting moments so I insisted on getting an EKG stress test on the treadmill. The cardiologist immediately detected a problem and after scheduling further tests asked if I hadn't felt any symptoms. When I related to him that my doctor had told me to "not worry about the chest pain, because I was in good shape" he told me I needed to change doctors.

Within days I learned that four of my arteries were 70% occluded and was scheduled for a quadruple bypass three weeks hence. I was told not to exercise during that period. When I told the cardiologist that I would be leaving for New Guinea in two days, he said, "No you're not." I said, "Yes, I am" and, of course, I did. On that trip I snorkeled for four hours a day. One day, walking back up the hill from the boat dock to the resort just a little too fast so as not to miss lunch, I felt a massive chest pain and had to stop and breathe slowly for almost five minutes before the angina attack subsided. It was scary. There was only one flight a week out of there and no hospitals in the country equipped for heart surgery.

The operation, itself, though, didn't really phase me and within a week I was walking two miles daily, six miles inside of a month. Being in good shape makes all the difference to a speedy recovery.

One of my swimmers welcomed me to the 10 Inch Club. I thought he was referring to my penis but he meant the scar on my chest. I wrote a team newsletter article about being more proactive when you suspect a health problem and received calls from quite a number of swimmers thanking me for prodding them to look after their health. Several were subsequently diagnosed with heart disease and had bypasses or stents put in.

Chapter XII
Singapore, 1998-99

While training the Malaysian swim team in early 1988, I met an American, a former swimmer at the University of Illinois, who had swam there with my best childhood friend. He actually lived and worked in Singapore but had a branch office in Kuala Lumpur, Malaysia. Kit's children swam on the club team at the Singapore American School and he offered me the coaching job there. I brought my personal effects to his office in KL to be shipped to Singapore. Chatting with his Malaysian-Chinese office manager, I invited her to dinner.

Mary became one of the loves of my life and, though she was married, we managed to meet, when possible, for 18 years. Her marriage was arranged by her parents but she did love her husband. For the first six years, we met in places like Greece, Alaska, Thailand, the Philippines and India. She would tell her husband she was traveling with a girlfriend. He actually took me out to lunch once, after Mary told him that I was an executive in her company. When she returned from Greece, he found a photo of me among the pictures of her trip. Recognizing me, he asked how it happened that I appeared in the photo. She replied that was a real coincidence, running into me in Greece.

The next year, she visited me in Alaska. I gave her the telephone number of one of my girl swimmers for her husband to call in case of an emergency. When he called, the airhead told him that she was at Rick's house. Then, realizing what she had just done, the girl called me. Mary then called her husband. For an hour, they were on the phone speaking

Chinese. When she hung up, I asked what the verdict was. She just said not to worry about it. To this day, I wonder what she told him.

In 1994, we met in India. After the trip, I mailed her copies of my photos and a letter. The envelope must have been torn because the photos and letter arrived at her house in a clear plastic bag provided by the post office. That day, her husband arrived home first and opened the bag, read my letter and gave her an ultimatum. She had to choose between him and me. She wrote me that she told him she loved us both and couldn't make that decision. Shortly after, I received the most amazing letter from her husband in which he wrote that if I was ever in Singapore he would "take care of me real quick" but if I were to apologize, maybe after a few months, the three of us could travel together!

I didn't reply but I still have the letter. It wasn't long until I got another letter from Mary telling me that she was breaking off our relationship. We had always made it clear that if the time came, that would be the realistic option.

Five years went by and, on a whim, I decided to locate her again. I asked one of my former Malaysian swimmers to get her telephone number from her parents. She had moved to Singapore with her husband. I called her from the Philippines, on my way to Singapore and she agreed to have dinner. After just a glance, all the great feelings came back and we resumed our clandestine meetings at hotels when I visited Singapore. This went on for another five years until she broke it off again, fearful that her growing children might find out about us.

So, I arrived in Singapore in August 1998 to begin the new season with the Singapore Fighting Fish, known to the swimmers as the Farting Fish. My assistant coach was a young Singaporean, the nicest guy you'd ever want to meet, who today decides which drug dealers live or die as the No. 2 person in the anti-narcotics bureau. When I arrived, I met with my friend Kit and the club president, another American, who represented the worst of the arrogant foreign business executives so common around the world. I presented them with my written program for the reorganization of the team. The president said he wouldn't accept my recommendations and they would continue with the previous system.

I countered that there wasn't any point in hiring a professional coach, the resident expert in the field, if they weren't going to respect his expertise. The president responded by slamming his fist on the table and shouting, "I'm the boss here and you will do as you are told."

Well, that wasn't about to happen. I told Kit that we needed to discuss this and soon the president resigned but Kit told me that his cronies on the board would get their revenge.

The expatriate community is quite large in business-oriented Singapore. The city-state itself is very impressive at first glance, with its pristine parks, clean streets, architecturally impressive skyscrapers and racial policies that have produced harmony among the majority Chinese and minority Malay and Indian segments of the population. Singapore professes to be a democracy, but in reality, it is a one-party state that allows no dissent. Foreign books and magazines critical of the government's policies are routinely banned.

Four months after I arrived in Singapore, we competed against the International School of Jakarta's team, a traditional annual rivalry. We lost against a much larger team but our swimmers had a great meet with 90 percent turning in personal best times. After the meet, I was told that I was responsible for the defeat and my contract was rescinded. One member of the board told me she voted against me because I hadn't taken her seven-year-old daughter's split in the 100 medley relay.

But I received dozens of letters of support from the swimmers' families. At a special board meeting, several of the angry parents demanded an explanation. One parent, a CIA agent in Singapore, asked if promoting excellence wasn't part of this board's agenda and was told point blank that it wasn't. During the meeting, held at the board president's home, his wife continually complained about the incompetence of their Filipino maids, who were standing right there next to the table. What a bitch! She characterized many ex-pats in host countries.

Within days, I received an invitation to coach the Singapore Swimming Club, the former British Officers Club of Singapore, which counted among its world class facilities two 50 meter pools. I stayed at the club working with the kids for about six weeks, building rapport, reorganizing the swimming department. We had a meet and the kids did really well, in fact, too well, as I soon found out. I went to the US for a short visit and on my return I was notified that the club was having some problems getting my work visa extended, but not to worry. As the weeks went by, the situation became grimmer and eventually I was told that I had 30 days to leave the country.

I was informed by a reliable source that the former police chief of Singapore who was the vice president of a rival club had used his pull to cancel my visa after my swimmers had done so well in the earlier meet. I called up a local newspaper reporter I knew to give him the scoop and he just laughed, "We can't print anything incriminating that guy. This is Singapore." The ex-police chief was a long time member of the FINA bureau.

Chapter XIII
Alaska, 1999-2004

Before I departed from Singapore, I applied for several jobs in the US, using the American Swimming Coaches Association Job Service. I shipped my things to my old Peace Corps friend Gary in Minneapolis and enjoyed his hospitality for a couple of weeks until I got a bite from a club in, of all the unlikely places, Anchorage, Alaska. I thought, well, let's try something different for six months and then move on. I never would have dreamed that I would be in that cold land for eight out of the next nine years. I arrived with my usual collection of shorts, sandals and t-shirts and immediately bought a whole new wardrobe. Within a month of my arrival, the first snow fell and it was 10 below zero before I knew what hit me.

No prude myself, as the reader has already figured out, I was still shocked when I began to coach my Alaskan swimmers, by the foul language so common among the kids and the lack of respect shown to the coaches. The worst of all were the hockey players. In the locker room, the 10 and under players told each other to get fucked, stick it up your ass, etc. as part of their normal conversation. And, you should have heard the parents screaming obscenities at the kids during the games. No wonder the children showed no respect for their elders.

I was hired by the University Swim Club, based at the University of Alaska, Anchorage pool. Within a few months, the coach of another club decided to immigrate to Australia and asked me if I was interested in merging the two teams. Of course I was and after a trial period, we all met at an elementary school one evening to choose a name for the new club. The kids were set on 'People in Swim Suits' because the acronym on the caps and shirts would be PISS. The parents nixed that one and we finally decided on Northern Lights Swim Club which would dominate Alaska swimming for the next nine years and more. As we walked out of the school that night and looked up, the northern lights were blazing overhead, the first time I had ever seen them. What a good omen.

People always say, "Swimming in Alaska? That's gotta be a joke." In spite of all the obvious disadvantages—the cold, the distance between towns, many isolated on islands with the only connection by air, the expense of flying everywhere, the lack of competition for the better swimmers, the attraction of the traditional winter sports like ice hockey, ice skating and skiing, we still had quite a successful program. From 1990 to 1998 we had at least one and often two Junior National West Top 16 finalists every year—one champion, Sarah Murphy, and one runner up, Sara Fallico, who also made the US National Junior Squad.

Both Sara and Sarah were Senior National qualifiers. Sara was a talented young lady who always made it clear that she detested swimming. She had her moments, though, when against her better judgment, her competitive side took over. At the Region XII Championshipsmeet in Federal Way, WA one year, she was not behind her block yet in the 100 fly when the referee sarcastically asked if the swimmer in the empty lane was going to join the others. Sara jumped up and proceeded to kick butt in what was not her best event. At Junior Nationals in Dallas in 1991, she tied for 8th with a 58.2 in the 100 back in the prelims. After destroying the other girl in the swim off with a 56.9, she said, "There was no way I was going to let that fat girl beat me. I was just unable to harness that spirit on a regular basis." She left swimming at the age of 16.

NLSC also had Top Ten finishes at the Far Western Championships in Northern California and the Region XII Age Group and Open Championships in Seattle. We were all proud of our accomplishments and the fact of proving the doubters wrong. As Senior Chair of Alaska Swimming, I was able to fund the travel expenses for all Junior and Senior National Qualifiers. There were about 25 swimming clubs in Alaska, scattered around a state twice the size of Texas and almost a three-hour flight from Seattle, the nearest city where we could find good competition.

Coaching around the world, I learned to be creative in motivating my swimmers. One of the prime reasons why kids swim is to travel. In Alaska, our state meets would rotate to different regions so everyone got a chance to travel and many clubs had the opportunity to host a meet. In addition to the official meets, I organized dual meets with clubs from towns two to three hours from Anchorage. We would charter a bus and stay overnight at the local high school, bringing sleeping bags, playing cards and watching videos all night. Obviously, the purpose of the meets was to have fun, not swim fast, but those little trips made a big difference to the kids and they looked forward to them.

Even more important, each summer, I would organize a two-week training trip to the Lower 48. We visited such places as Chicago, St Louis, Minneapolis, Fullerton, Long Beach and Ventura, housing with the host team's families, visiting all the famous tourist sites in the area and competing in one or two meets. I would take up to 20 swimmers, with no chaperones, and we never had a problem.

What really kept me in Alaska all those years was the high school season. During the three month season, from mid-August to mid-November, all the older swimmers were required to train with their high school coaches. This freed me up to travel and I would go around the world, giving clinics, visiting old friends.

Alaska, though remote, still had its politics. The chairwoman of our Anchorage area local swimming committee, Sue Brown, was a rather large overbearing woman from our main rival, the Aurora Swim Club. At the state championships one summer, both Sara Fallico and I were interviewed by a local newspaper. When asked who her biggest competition came from, we both responded that it came at meets in the Lower 48, not in Alaska, where she dominated her events.

The article came out on Sunday, the last day of the meet. I was on deck warming up the swimmers when Sue came up to me and, in front of several other parents, said, "I saw your comments in the newspaper. You are so full of shit." I was temporarily speechless. My first thought was that the journalist had misquoted me so I went to someone in the stands who had a newspaper and scanned the article. It was exactly as I had dictated. I then decided that she wasn't going to get away with that and went back to Sue and told her that she was full of shit, too, but just in a much larger quantity.

We didn't speak again for six months. Then, one weekend, at home, the phone rang and a young lady asked if she could train with my club and that she was one of the top swimmers in Alaska. I asked who she was and she said Molly Brown, Sue's daughter.

I said, "Yeah, sure. Who are you?"

She said again, Molly Brown. Still thinking it was a prank, I asked, in my most sarcastic tone, "Does your mother know you are calling?" She said her mom told her she was old enough to make her own decisions.

I apologized for my mistake. Both Molly and her sister joined NLSC and that summer made up half of our medley relay that qualified for Senior Nationals. Sue even hosted pancake breakfasts for the team at her house and we ended up, if not friends, at least with respect for each other.

As the state meets rotated, every couple of years we would have a meet in Fairbanks, in February. I was always amazed at how the local residents would defend their town as being a great place to live. I thought it had no redeeming factors. We would stay at a nice hotel with a kitchenette about a block and a half from a supermarket and I remember walking out of the hotel to buy some food at 38 below zero.

At first you couldn't breathe deeply because it felt like your lungs were searing. You would sip some air into your mouth, and hold it in to warm up before taking it down into your lungs. In addition, at that temperature, carbon monoxide from car emissions crystallizes and forms very visible layers in the air. You would get a mouthful of the stuff as you walked. It wasn't fun. We would run to the store and spend five minutes warming up before we could shop. Going back was even worse, when we were loaded down with shopping bags.

In my fifth year coaching NLSC, a new president of the board was elected. That night, his wife called me at home and said, "Now that my husband is president we will expect you to give more attention to our children." Classic stuff. I told her not to hold her breath waiting for that to happen.

Soon, my annual evaluation came up. Each family received an evaluation form to fill out rating the head coach in a number of areas which determined a portion of my annual bonus of up to 10 percent of my salary. The new president's wife rounded up a couple of cronies and they gave me a low rating in several areas, including punctuality and attendance though I had never been either absent or late. That year was our most successful, having won all the state championships, both Senior and Age Group, by a large margin. When the time came to pay my reduced bonus, the president informed me that the club didn't have any money available and I wouldn't receive anything at all.

It was, once again, time to move on. I had received a call from the Ohio State University coach, Bill Wadley, about an opening with the National Team of Kuwait and was told it was mine for the taking. I sent my résumé' to the Kuwaitis, revising it to leave no indication that I had coached in Israel and, after a perfunctory interview in New York City, I was offered the job.

Chapter XIV
Kuwait, 1994-95

Kuwait is not a tourist destination. In fact, you could not even enter the country as a tourist, at least when I lived there. A work visa was required and that excluded atheists and persons with AIDS. I couldn't even bring in a girlfriend to visit unless she was my wife. There are 600,000 Kuwaitis but about two million foreign workers. When a Kuwaiti male finishes high school, more often than not by bribing his foreign teachers to allow him to pass, he is guaranteed a civil service position by the government. Then, he hires a person from a third world country to do the job, paying him about a tenth of the salary he receives.

At the time I lived in Kuwait, a single male could not rent an apartment until he married. The vast majority of marriages were arranged by parents, often marrying their children to their cousins. After marriage, the couple was then eligible for a $250,000 low interest loan to buy or build their home. There were no movie theaters in the country, nowhere to dance or listen to music. In some restaurants, single males were required to sit in a separate room so they couldn't see the married women unveiled. Women are not required by law to be veiled or wear the full length robes but most of them are mandated by their husbands to do so.

Unlike in the Emirates where real efforts were made to beautify the landscape with trees and parks, Kuwait City was just desert and mansions with an unattractive downtown business and hotel area. The city is divided by five north-south and east-west freeways into large square blocks. Each block is a semi-independent area with schools, a shopping area and residential buildings.

When I began my new job, I left Alaska and met up in St. Louis with the four Kuwaiti swimmers who were to train with me in preparation for the Asian Games in Hiroshima, five months hence. I was asked to find places for them to train overseas because in Kuwait they wouldn't train seriously, if at all. I received a check for $25,000 and instructions to request more when needed. I was also asked to keep the receipts for major expenses such as hotels, airline tickets and car rentals but, whenever possible, try to get falsified receipts increasing the actual cost so reimbursement would be greater than expense.

We began our training odyssey in Carbondale, Illinois. The first three weeks were spent swimming with the Southern Illinois University swimming teams. It was fun to return and visit with some old friends again and the guys had the opportunity to train with and be motivated by the SIU swimmers.

When we checked out before going to the airport heading to Orlando, I got my first shock. Entering the hotel rooms of the swimmers, I found cases of Coca Cola, enough food to feed an army, a table piled with coins, all left behind. I was beginning to comprehend that these spoiled people had no sense of value. We would often have breakfast at a Denny's restaurant where the menu shows all the grand slam breakfasts with prices ranging from $3 to $5. The Kuwaitis would ask for each item to be put on an individual plate, tripling the price. When shopping at a mall and confronted with the same item in two different shops at different prices, they had no qualms about buying the more expensive one.

One of my swimmers asked if I could loan him some money. What happened to yours, I asked. He had spent $2,500 on phone calls to his friends in Kuwait. At one of our hotels, the laundry machines were free. The Kuwaitis, though, wouldn't think of doing their own laundry. They took everything to the dry cleaners.

We trained in Orlando for two weeks then drove down to Fort Lauderdale to compete in the Alamo invitational. There were several swimmers from foreign teams, including the national team of Cuba. I introduced myself to the Cuban coach and it turned out he had been a participant in the clinic I gave in Havana 15 years earlier. The local newspaper interviewed me for an article on the differences between the Cuban team, the poorest in the league, and the Kuwaiti team, the wealthiest. On Sunday morning, the article appeared and when I arrived at the pool, Jack Nelson, the host team coach told me someone was looking for me. He pointed him out and as I went over, I recognized a swimmer from my very first team in Ecuador.

Juan had seen the article and wanted me to meet his two kids. An hour later, another former swimmer from Ecuador who had also seen the article and now, too, lived in the area showed up. We had a nice reunion dinner that night.

At the meet, the Kuwaiti team was scheduled to compete in the 800 free relay. Because there were only two men's and two women's relays in the slow heat, the heats were combined. As I walked up to the staging area to give the guys some last minute advice, they told me they refused to swim with women. I told them, "Then, you will be on a plane back to Kuwait tomorrow." They swam.

Our next stop was Somerset Hills, New Jersey where another coaching friend had invited us to spend two weeks training with his team. The Kuwaitis insisted on renting a limo from Kennedy airport to NJ. It was the limo ride from hell. I had never been in a limo before and didn't realize there was virtually no space in the trunk. Among the five of us we had 16 full-size suitcases and about 10 smaller bags. By the time the luggage was creatively stacked inside the limo, it left only enough room for four of us to sit with our legs out the windows and the 5th lying on his back on top of the suitcases with his nose an inch from the roof. Then, in NJ, when we went to rent a car, the only thing we could find that day was two junks at Rent a Wreck. The guys' car had no aircon. I kind of chuckled to myself seeing their discomfort. After New Jersey, we finally went to Kuwait. I had a FINA clinic scheduled for the Persian Gulf coaches in Kuwait City and soon after, we would go to Dubai for the Persian Gulf Championships.

In Kuwait I was assigned a driver, an Indian Muslim. He was one of those holier-than-thou types. During the month of Ramadan, when Muslims don't eat from dawn to dusk, he took it one step further, by not even swallowing his saliva. He would accumulate this big saliva wad in his mouth, then pull over and spit it out in the street. He wasn't all that he seemed to be, though, and had no qualms about stealing money from me, an expensive pair of binoculars and going through my photographs when I was away, taking the ones of scantily-clad women. He also regularly informed on me to my boss, when I said anything negative about Kuwait.

The clinic was interesting. We were supposed to go from seven to 10 in the evening but since the evening prayers began at 7:30, the coaches decided there was no point starting at 7, so we cut an hour off each session. I was a little upset over this but no one else seemed to mind.

The meet in Dubai was in both age group and open divisions. After we arrived the other countries saw that we had the strongest senior team, so they decided to cancel the open events. That old motto again: "Better not to compete, than to risk losing face."

In the middle of finals the first evening, everyone began to leave the pool. I asked what was going on and, of course, it was time for evening prayers. The meet was delayed about an hour every night. We returned to Kuwait bringing back quite a bit of Duty Free booze. One of the swimmers had a cousin who was a customs official and he waved us through. On other occasions, I would buy a two-liter bottle of 7-Up and carefully remove the cap without breaking the seal, dump out the soda and refill it with gin or vodka, then reseal it. I always got the sneer from customs officials, "Stupid American, carrying a bottle of 7-Up all this way when he can buy it here."

I lived in an apartment building exclusively for foreign coaches. There were 16 of us, all specialists in a variety of sports and mostly from Russia or the former Soviet Republics. Many of the coaches barely worked at all. Some had been in Kuwait for seven or eight years. They didn't complain because with the collapse of the Soviet Union, the government no longer paid them. Working in Kuwait was a bonanza and they could support many family members back home on their salaries.

I finally figured out that we were little more than trophies to brag about among the Persian Gulf rulers. The Saudis could say, "We have the famous fencing coach," the Kuwaitis could counter, "Well, we have the famous diving coach." It wasn't important that there were no fencers or divers. The Russian coaches were masters at making bathtub booze out of any fruit or vegetable that could be fermented. After being trapped in the elevator with them, I wondered when they bathed, though.

I saw a young couple moving into the apartment below mine. A couple of days later, I needed a hammer and knocked on their door to borrow one. No one answered, but I could see movement through the peep hole in the door. I knocked again and the door cracked open, and a woman's face appeared. I asked if she had a hammer. She didn't appear to understand so I asked again very slowly and gestured to show what I needed. In broken English, she told me she was happy that her husband, an Egyptian tennis coach, wasn't home. She brought me a hammer and told me to leave quickly because her brother-in-law was always spot-checking on her. She was forbidden to leave the apartment when her husband was traveling, often for weeks at a time so, the brother-in-law did her shopping when needed.

After Dubai, we spent a few days in Kuwait before departing for the next stage of our training camp, at Crystal Palace, just outside of London. For this camp, we had all the age groups and their individual coaches, as well. After checking into our fancy hotel near Buckingham Palace, I was called by the head of the delegation and asked to come to his room. As I walked in, he shut the door and opened a closet door. "If you need anything, just let me know." The closet was stacked with cases of beer, bottles of wine, scotch, gin, vodka. We were only staying for two weeks. You gotta love those pious Muslims.

We would leave the hotel each morning at about 9 for the one-hour drive to Crystal Palace in our chartered bus. One of my four senior swimmers never made it on time for the morning sessions. I gave him an ultimatum and the federation supported me and sent him home. He immediately went on a radio show lambasting the American coach who didn't know anything about coaching. The federation replaced him with another senior swimmer who hadn't been training for over a year.

When the two weeks were up, the age groupers returned to Kuwait and I headed to Hania, Crete with four senior swimmers, ages 18 to 25, to continue training and to compete in the Greek summer national championships. We stayed in a hotel only six blocks from the pool. I walked but the swimmers took taxis every day. The water is warm in the summer in Greece and the swimmers hated it there. They said it was too much like home. So, after the nationals, we cut it short and returned to London to continue training at the Crystal Palace pool.

The swimmers liked London because there is a large Kuwaiti community there. In fact, there is a "Little Kuwait" area where thousands of Kuwaitis have apartments, the shops are owned by Kuwaitis and signs are written in Arabic. One day, walking in that district, three limos pulled up to the curb. The first had the mother and father, the second, the two kids and the maid and the third was full of the packages they had bought.

We went to a café where the Kuwaitis hang out. One table would be full of guys, the next full of girls. They would exchange sultry glances but never mix. One of the guys told me that he was going to take a vacation and would meet up with us later. I had him kicked off the team and they sent me another one, who hadn't been in the water for over a year and had been suspended for throwing the former American coach, Steve Betts against a wall. Then my best swimmer told me he had to go to Saudi Arabia with his dad to meet his future wife, a first cousin. I asked, "Can't it wait until after the games?" No, so he disappeared for 10 days, too.

Our next stop was Singapore. A Kuwaiti manager joined us for this portion of the trip. His job was to organize everything we needed but he called me to his room the first day and asked if I could take care of everything. If I really needed something, I could call him. He mentioned that his wife was expecting their first child. Then he asked if I could arrange women for him or a sex trip to Bangkok. I said he would have to do that on his own. Pimping was not about to be on my résumé'.

I went to his room only once all the time we were there. He had a metallic carpet in the middle of the living room in his suite with his hubbly-bubbly water pipe set up. The room smelled so bad, I had to leave quickly. We spent another two weeks in that shoppers' paradise and the guys did enjoy it there. We stayed at a very fancy hotel and I was able to meet up with my lovely Malaysian girlfriend who was then living in Singapore.

We trained at the very fancy Chinese Swimming Club where I had given clinics in the past. At practice one afternoon, one of the guys asked if he could go to the bathroom. I said, of course, and he got out. In no time, he was back complaining that there was no hose in the stall. I said here people use toilet paper just like in London. The Kuwaitis wipe with their hand and water from the hose. That is why the Muslims will never shake your left hand, because you eat with the right, wipe with the left. So, the boy went back and finally returned to finish practice.

After practice, they went to the hotel while I remained and enjoyed a swim. Entering the locker room after my swim, I opened the first shower stall and couldn't believe what I saw—a large turd on the floor. The Kuwaiti had taken a shit in the shower. This was a very exclusive club. How embarrassing. At this point two more of the swimmers left the training camp and returned to Kuwait to take entrance exams for school. They would meet us in Japan, missing the whole taper.

The last phase of the training camp was to be in Seoul, South Korea but just a day before departure, I received a call from Kuwait informing me that because of a major holiday in South Korea, all the pools would be closed for four days. We had to extend our stay four more days in Singapore. I went to the hotel manager and asked to extend our reservation. He said that, unfortunately, the hotel was fully booked the following day but after that, we could return. He recommended another nice hotel just two blocks away. I went to check it out, made the reservation and the next day we switched.

As we walked in, the swimmer who had shit in the shower said, "I'm not staying here!"

I asked him why and he responded that the lobby was too small. I gave him the choice of a park bench or that hotel for one night. The day came to leave for South Korea and we took two cabs to the airport. The manager smelled so bad that I was afraid they wouldn't let him on the plane. To this day I believe that he never bathed the whole time we were there. I took everyone's tickets to the counter to get our boarding passes and requested a seat for myself on the opposite side of the plane from the rest of the guys. As we boarded, the stewardess who checked our tickets as we entered the plane almost fell backwards as the stench of the manager hit her. I was following and whispered "Can you believe that?"

She said, "In all my years, I have never smelled anything so foul."

In Seoul, we stayed in a hotel that had a miniature Disneyland connected to it. We were there for only five days, then on to Hiroshima. So here I was at the Asian Games with this mish-mash group of swimmers, none of whom had trained properly for a meet of this magnitude. The night before the swimming events began, the sheik, head of the delegation, really psyched the swimmers up by promising a new Mercedes to any who won gold medals. What a joke that was but the guys really thought it could happen, God willing, as they would always say. I once told them that in the States, people say, "God helps those who help themselves" and showing up to practice once in a while might make a difference. But I was preaching to deaf ears.

Predictably, once the meet was underway, my swimmers didn't swim up to expectations. The night before the final day's events, the new guy who had attacked the former coach tried to grab me but was held back by two other swimmers. My assistant coach, a Kuwaiti who wanted my job, didn't even come to my aid. The swimmer was, once again, suspended. Back in Kuwait, at a meeting of the Kuwaiti Olympic Committee members to discuss the Asian Games failure, my assistant told them that the American coach doesn't know how to taper swimmers who don't train. What a class act he was.

I was surprised in Hiroshima to find out that the head of the sports organization that controls sports in Asia was a Kuwaiti sheik. How could this tiny country with such a weak sports tradition be in command of a region with such traditional powers as China, Japan and South Korea? One day, hanging out at the swimming federation office, I read a letter sitting open on a desk. It was from the Olympic Committee of Nepal and it thanked the Kuwaitis for funding all the membership fees required to remain in good standing with the international sports organizations. I asked the secretary about it and he said, "Sure, how do you think we get their votes at election time? We do that for all the poor nations in the region and they, in turn, vote for our candidates."

My former boss in Kuwait is now a FINA bureau member. I wonder how that happened.

When I departed on a six-week vacation, I was sure that they would cancel my contract. Truthfully, there was little reason for me to be there, but when I returned, no one said anything and I began the new season. I was then told that they were unable to get my visa arranged in Kuwait and I would have to go to the Kuwaiti Embassy in Washington. Well, that just meant another two weeks of vacation.

Finally, now legal, I was ready to begin coaching again. But arriving at the pool where we trained, I found it locked. The manager said that someone had shit in the pool and he was going to teach us a lesson by locking us out for a week.

I asked my boss about the meet schedule for the coming year. He said nothing was scheduled. I asked how he expected to motivate these guys to train if there is nothing to look forward to? So, he scheduled a meet in Iran. I was very excited about the opportunity to visit a country I most likely would never go to because of the political situation. At the Asian Games, I was introduced to the Iranian coach and he was very friendly and even gave me some gifts and introduced me to all his swimmers.

The night before we departed for Iran, the trip was cancelled because the Olympic committee in some political wrangling with the swimming federation officials, only gave tickets for the swimmers but none for coaches or officials. I asked, "What next?"

They arranged a meet in Bahrain, the island off the coast of Saudi Arabia where alcohol is legal, and to which the Saudis built the world's longest causeway so they could drive over to drink there. We checked into our hotel with about 40 swimmers and went to the pool only to find out that the heating system had been broken for months. We had a very short meet in very cold water and then went shopping for four days. One day, as I was about to leave the hotel for a walk, I noticed all the kids, 10 to 13 years old, hanging around the lobby. I asked what they were up to and they said, as usual, on the trips, the coaches would disappear telling them not to leave the hotel. I said, "Alright, everybody can come with me." I took them shopping and sightseeing. They, and later their parents, were so grateful.

Back from that debacle, I prodded the federation to arrange a real meet for the swimmers. It was announced that we would go to Egypt and swim against its national team. This time, we had 80 in the delegation including age groupers, water polo players and a large number of "officials" who went along for the free ride. Arriving in the Cairo airport, I was a bit apprehensive when no one showed up to meet us. I suggested to one of the guys that it might be a good idea to call the Egyptian Swim Federation office. He did and it turned out the Egyptians didn't know we were coming. No one had bothered to inform them.

Scrambling at the last minute, we were able to arrange a time trials with one of the local clubs. I did have the opportunity to take the swimmers around to see the fabulous sights of Cairo, if nothing else.

No one but I was upset about the latest fuck-up so I figured that it was about time to call it a day for Kuwait. By that time, virtually no one of my national swimmers would show up to train. He who had shit in the shower came to the pool one day. I hadn't seen him in a month. He arrived a half hour late and said, "Coach, I have to leave early today."

"How much time do you have?"

"Just 45 minutes."

"Ok, do a 400 warm-up and 20x 100 on 1:30." I timed his set and after 13, he stopped and got out.

"Where are you going?" I asked.

"I'm finished," he replied.

"You did 20?"

"Who's counting, coach?"

That was the last time I ever saw him. The coach of the 10 and under group was another winner. When the kids arrived at the pool, they would ask, "What to do, coach?" and he would say, "Swim a thousand," then sit down and read his newspaper.

Next, the kids would ask, "What now, coach?" Swim a thousand," as he went into the stands to chat on his cell phone. Finally, swim a thousand, again, as he sat in the stands to converse with the parents.

I finally said to my boss, "Look, the coach of the 10 and unders, who should be building the base for us, teaching stroke mechanics to these kids, doesn't do anything."

He replied, "We all know that but he is married to a princess from the royal family, so there is nothing we can do."

Out of boredom, I took a group of five 11, 12 and 13-year olds who no one really paid attention to because they weren't very good. In six weeks, they had improved so much that their coaches took them away from me. Since my swimmers rarely showed up, I spent my days jogging in the morning, lifting at the nearby gym at noon and swimming in the evening. I lost 15 pounds and was physically in the best shape since college, but mentally, I couldn't stand another day there. Every morning, the chant from the mosque's loud speakers calling the faithful to prayers blasted me awake at about 4:30. Watching movies on TV, they were invariably interrupted by the prayer sessions and once the prayer ended, the movie didn't resume, so every day you only saw half of a movie.

I met a guy at the gym who was very friendly and I would see him there every day. I asked him if he had a job. His reply characterized the corruption rampant in Kuwaiti society. He had gone to a US university and earned a Masters degree in engineering. Returning home, he was assigned a job with the department of highways. After several months, he began to be suspicious of large amounts of money that couldn't be accounted for and alerted his boss. His boss thanked him and said he would get back to him. A week later, he was called in to a meeting of the department heads, given the keys to a new Mercedes, and told not to come back to work again. He received his regular salary and annual raises but never had to report for work. Some guys have all the luck.

He invited me to his "country" home one weekend. There is a region of Kuwait about an hour from Kuwait City near the Saudi border that has enough ground water to support light agriculture. Many Kuwaitis have built homes there and have vegetable gardens and the traditional Bedouin tent in the back yard to maintain a connection with their cultural past. That night, a half dozen of my friend's male neighbors (the men escape to this place but don't bring the women) gathered in his back yard sitting around the camp fire and sipping scotch. One by one, they disappeared into the tent until only my friend and I were left outside. I asked if we should join the others and he reluctantly agreed. We entered, and much to my surprise, found that they were smoking hash. My friend was happy that I was okay with that and passed the pipe to me.

The treatment of women in Muslim countries is a big issue for me. One afternoon, I walked into the pool to find one of the moms arguing with the pool manager. She was an Iranian woman who had married a Kuwaiti and was able to get a divorce, almost unheard of when instigated by a woman. Her husband was such a blatant asshole that even the Kuwaiti judge could not ignore his abuse. I went up to her and asked what all the fuss was about. She spoke excellent English and explained that the manager had just decided that women would no longer be allowed to enter the pool. I told the guy to fuck off and took her arm, escorting her to the stands.

Not long after, I heard shouting in the lobby. The manager tried to prevent another woman, also foreign and married to a Kuwaiti, from entering. I also escorted her inside and discovered she was from a South American country so we could speak Spanish. Not more than a few minutes passed and again, I heard shouting from the lobby. This time it was a Kuwaiti woman who had lived in the US for years. She was giving back everything she got from the manager and I brought her in, too. The Kuwaiti coaches were really pissed at me and said it was none of my business to interfere. I told them if they had any common decency they would have been out there helping the women.

In London, on one of our trips, I was appalled to see my assistant coach's wife cutting his meat for him in bite-sized pieces and having her dinner only after he finished eating. One day, he lamented that in his father's time, the women walked three steps behind the men, but now they brazenly walk next to their husbands.

I later met the South American mom, clandestinely, for walks and she told me of the horrible life she led in Kuwait. She was from a wealthy family, had met this millionaire in London who had swept her off her feet, but after marriage and moving to Kuwait, he began to beat and publicly humiliate her. I asked why she didn't leave and she said that she didn't want to leave her kids. The older boy, then about 11, was already calling her a whore, mimicking her husband. The younger boy was just eight. She received no allowance from her husband and was on anti-depressants just to make it through the day. I have no idea what happened to her.

In Kuwait, the wife may only depart the country with her children if the husband gives written permission. If the husband dies, his family, not his wife, gets custody of the children. A foreigner, even if married to a Kuwaiti, cannot attain Kuwaiti citizenship. When a man divorces his wife, he is not expected to pay alimony.

I acquired an absolute disdain for the Muslim religion after my year in Kuwait. But the Kuwaiti women were not at the bottom of the heap. That honor was reserved for the foreign maids, all from poor countries, who were treated almost like slaves. They typically worked 10 hour days, seven days a week. Often they were subjected to sexual abuse by the Kuwaiti men and beaten by the Kuwaiti women, who had no one else they could lord it over. One headline in the local English language newspaper read, "Kuwaiti woman fined $1,500 for beating her maid to death."

I had noticed some of the Muslim men with black smudges on their foreheads and was told they were the most devout Muslims and the smudge came from banging their heads so hard on their prayer rugs. On a trip to Egypt, I even saw some with indented foreheads. I bet they got first class treatment in heaven.

I noticed my swimmers didn't like dogs and would actually run away from them. I asked one of the guys if he was scared of dogs when he ran away from a little cocker spaniel. He said dogs were unclean and shouldn't touch you. But I guess wiping your ass with your hand was ok, even if a little bit of shit remained under your finger nails.

Another of the Kuwaitis' endearing habits was to pull up in front of a building and honk their car horn until their friend came down. This could be as long as 15-20 minutes of non-stop honking any time, day or night. Driving in Kuwait was another nightmare. Few people used turn signals, many initiated turns from the wrong lane. People double parked, facing the wrong way, ignored stop signs and, of course, considered pedestrians fair game.

Women were not permitted to shake hands with a man unless he was from the immediate family. I learned that the hard way in the airport when I stretched out my hand to greet the mother of one of my swimmers and someone passing by whacked my arm and began screaming at me.

In order not to pay US taxes on your overseas earnings, you must stay outside the US for 11 months. I waited 11 months and one day before getting my butt out of Kuwait. Every day seemed like a month, though. I had stayed in touch with one of the parents of my Alaska team, a former club president. When the club did a search for a new coach after I left, they consulted with me for input about the candidates. I told them they should check some references for the candidate they decided upon but it didn't happen.

What happened was that they had hired an alcoholic. He didn't last very long. He would get seriously stressed before swim meets and not show up. The parents went to his house to find him dead drunk on the floor. He was fired and only a couple of years later, succumbed to liver disease. Knowing I wasn't happy in Kuwait, I was asked if I would consider returning to Alaska. I said we had some unfinished business, the bonus the club didn't pay from the previous year. They agreed to pay it and I signed a new contract.

I was asked by several Kuwaitis before I departed if I wasn't earning enough money there. I told them that one thing I learned during my year in Kuwait was that money isn't everything. If I can't enjoy my job, then the money becomes meaningless. For people who generally don't work at all and whose idea of a good time is to spend every weekend at their father's house watching videos, I guess it was difficult to understand my response.

Chapter XV
Alaska, Part II, 1995-98

After the chaotic period that my former club went through when I departed, I was welcomed back with open arms and high expectations. We had a brief but very successful summer season and the following year, we continued on a high with a great trip to St. Louis and our first ever Junior National Champion, Sarah Murphy. On the St. Louis trip, we went with our host team to the town of Quincy, IL on the bank of the Mississippi River for their annual invitational swim meet. The host team did a great job of organizing the meet and the swimmers from Alaska were treated like royalty by the host families.

Over the next two years, I stayed in touch with the guy who had housed me. One morning during the second week of the trip, the swimmers arrived for practice looking somewhat hung over. The St. Louis team coach discovered that his kids had taken ours to a party the previous night and many had gotten drunk. He decided to teach them a lesson and had them swim 600 meters of freestyle with a flip turn after every 10 strokes. In no time, everyone was puking in the bushes.

During my years in Alaska, not only did I bring in foreign swimmers through the student exchange programs for my club, I also made myself available whenever Brazilian exchange students arrived to help them through homesickness. Being able to speak your own language again makes a big difference. At dinner one evening, I asked one of the Brazilian girls what her father did. Oh, he is a *maraja*, she replied. A *maraja* is a corrupt government official who got rich by stealing from the government. He built three hotels with the money he embezzled, she continued. I told her that I would be going to Brazil soon and if she wished, I would be happy to take a package for her family.

She packed a box of things and gave me her father's telephone number in the beach resort town of Porto Seguro. Arriving in Sao Paulo, I called her dad and he had a relative who was living in Sao Paulo pick up the package but he also told me that any time I came to Porto Seguro I would be welcome to stay at one of his hotels.

Two years later, I did exactly that. At first, he said he didn't remember the offer but then, with obvious reluctance in his voice, he told me to fly up. When I met him on the beach, he had a beer in one hand, a cigarette in the other and a large belly, obviously leading the good life. He was a federal congressman and it was obvious that he couldn't have built those hotels on his salary. But I had a nice vacation so I shouldn't complain too much.

Another of my Brazilian friends who worked for the government for many years told me the classic story of the Minister of the Interior responsible for protecting wildlife, who shipped a whole plane load of skins of endangered species to be sold in the black market in Europe.

I was getting tired of the cold weather in Alaska and to exacerbate things, my top swimmer came down with asthma and for the next year was rarely able to push herself at practice. She would get frustrated and down on herself and that affected the other swimmers, as well. It was tough, too, for the kids to do early morning practices in the winter when the temperature was hovering near zero and black ice covered the roads. We swam from 5 to 6:15 AM because school began early.

One of my swimmers, Jason, a decent breaststroker who was just tenths of a second from the Junior National cutoff time, never made it to the morning sessions. For the umpteenth time, I ragged him about it and he replied, "Coach, it is not important that I don't come, what is important is that I have the intention of coming." Needless to say he never made Juniors.

One of the things I had a difficult time comprehending, as I am sure is the case with many club coaches, was how the swimmers often swam faster during the short high school season with substandard training than they did during the much longer and more intensive club season. I was to finally figure that out in my next job. I began looking around for a new position in the beginning of 1998. As I mentioned, I had stayed in touch with a guy from the board of directors of the team in Quincy, Illinois and told him that I was looking to leave Alaska. He was very enthusiastic about the possibility of bringing me to Quincy and got the ball rolling. One of my major concerns was to not lose the kids during the high school season so, I asked him to try and make it a package deal, coaching both the club and high school teams. When the high school agreed, I signed the contract.

Chapter XVI
Quincy, Illinois, A Bad Aura, 1998-2000

In 1965, after completing my junior year, I attended summer quarter at Eastern Illinois University to take a class I needed to graduate but couldn't fit in during my senior year. We had several swimmers in school that summer and we trained together and went to an invitational meet in Quincy, Illinois, on the eastern bank of the Mississippi River across from Mark Twain's Hannibal, Missouri. I found a beautiful beach towel unattended in the pool locker room and stuffed it in my bag. I had that towel for 10 years until it was stolen on the beach in Rio. In a classic retribution story, this chapter might convince the reader that crime does not pay. I'm not sure, though, that one stolen towel could be the cause of all the disasters that follow.

So, in the summer of 1998, I shipped my personal belongings to Quincy and spent 10 days there before leaving for a trip to Africa. I planned to return at the end of August to begin the girls' high school season. On only my third day in Quincy, I was at my host's home when we got a call that the indoor swimming pool at the club had just been destroyed by a tornado, the first to hit Quincy in 60 years. Virtually nothing else was touched, only the pool. I had left the pool about 30 minutes earlier. I should have figured out then that it wasn't meant to be the place for me. Fortunately, 1) the club also had a 50m outdoor pool, and 2) the club had just recently renewed its insurance coverage which ended up paying for the damage.

I called the Illinois High School Association which oversees all high school sports in the state to find out some of their rules since I was coaching both the club and HS teams. The woman I talked to seemed knowledgeable, said she was the No.2 person in the department and told me that club coaches could not train the HS swimmers in the same pool at the same time. I explained that similar to other small towns in Illinois where only one pool was available, and in our case, owned by the club, we had no other option but to train together. She said she understood and to "just do the best you can."

On the first day of HS practice, I gave the girls the written guidelines for the new season. The team had been coached for the previous 17 years by a PE teacher who wasn't big on attendance or punctuality and had little knowledge of training methods. When one of the girls notified me that she had a job and would only be attending a couple of practices a week, I told her she could not be on the team. I called a parents' meeting and told them the rules. One parent asked if I was following the rules. I had no clue what he was referring to and replied that, yes, I was. He repeated his question in a very aggressive manner and, again, I said yes. After the meeting, his wife said her daughter had given up pom-pom girls for the swim team that year.

Bear in mind that as you enter Quincy, there is one of those signs on the highway notifying everyone that Quincy was the state HS champion pom-pom team in whenever. A rather meager claim to fame, some would say, but obviously a big deal to the locals. The ex-pom-pom girl, who was one of my team captains, came down sick for several days and missed practice. I told her to do the scheduled make-up practice on Sunday afternoon but she didn't show up and when I confronted her on Monday, in a flippant manner, she said she'd gone shopping with her grandmother.

To teach her a lesson, I didn't enter her in that week's dual meet. Her father, who we will call Mr. T, threw a fit and demanded that the school principal fire me immediately. The principal backed me up. I was then notified by the athletic director that there was a class I needed to take in Illinois for all new HS coaches. It was a basic class for entry level coaches and was the reason the aggressive parent, Mr. T, at the parents meeting asked if I had followed the rules. The AD had never told me about it so I was asked to hurriedly sign up for the next session, the following Saturday.

I could have taught that class. It was a take-home test type of class. I mailed in the result sheet and was informed a week later that I had flunked with only 30% correct answers but for $15 more, I could retake the test. I was pissed. It was impossible to flunk. So, since it was 90% true/false questions I just switched my answers from true to false and vice versa. Now, I had to pass. No! Again they said I had scored only 30%. I then called up the testing office and after complaining vigorously, I was told they must have made a mistake and they would send my diploma and refund my $15. So, now I was legal. What a joke!

I was then told by one of the other parents that Mr. T, who hadn't held a job in almost 10 years, had been calling up members of the school board trying to get me fired. Meanwhile, one of my best swimmers came down with toxic shock syndrome which affects about one in two million women and was in ICU at the local hospital for a week. We had a pretty weak team as it was and couldn't afford to lose anyone. Fortunately, the girl recovered but it was too late to help us that season. Another girl,13, kept blacking out at practice and eventually, was diagnosed with schizophrenia.

The season began to wind down and the night before the sectional championship in Springfield, we had the traditional pasta feed and I gave the girls their pre-meet massages in the home of a federal judge, the father of our other team captain. The next day, we had a decent meet, all things considered. Mr. T would call his daughter over for final instructions before her events. I mentioned it to her and she said, jokingly, "Well, at least this time he said almost the same thing you did." No one qualified for the state meet, so the season was over and the boys' season was about to begin.

The boys were far worse than the girls. Only one of the six was a year-round swimmer. Three were HS football players whose coach wanted them to stay in shape during the off season. One lineman weighed about 300 lbs. Though they were all nice kids, they weren't swimmers. At one practice, the 300-pounder started hyperventilating and passed out holding on to the wall. When the fire department arrived, it took about six firemen to pull him out. He had never worn a Speedo suit and refused to do so. I finally found one large enough but when he put it on he would walk around with a towel around his waist, sit on the edge of the pool and slide in while removing his towel.

A couple of weeks into the boys' season, my lawyer called me and said we had to go to a school board meeting to answer accusations of sexual abuse made by Mr. T who was still trying to get me fired. He alleged that I had inappropriately touched his daughter during the massage—only his daughter, and in a room with other swimmers present in the federal judge's house. He gave his spiel and then I gave my explanation with my lawyer. The next day, I was rehired for the coming year. This, of course, infuriated Mr. T who then sued me and all the members of the school board for $50,000 each in federal court.

When the Thanksgiving break came, I made it clear to the boys that they had to do double practices during the holidays. I kept precise attendance records and only one swimmer even came close to meeting the training requirement. After the holidays, I told the boys they had forfeited their right to go to the sectional meet, relenting in the case of the year-round swimmer who had made some of the practices. When one of the moms came in to complain, I showed her the attendance sheet but she wasn't interested in the facts and so, I made another enemy. Also, that fall, a lawyer for USA Swimming called and said they received information from someone that I had abused a minor. I explained the situation. They interviewed several people in Quincy before dropping the investigation. Everyone nowadays is covering their asses. USA Swimming had no business getting involved since the allegations concerned the HS season, not the club season.

One day, one of girls on the team called Mr. T's daughter and asked her why she was doing this. Mr. T then proceeded to try and sue the girl for $10,000, for harassment but that was soon dismissed. In the meantime, the club team was doing fine. I had several talented eighth grade girls who would, I believed, make the following year's HS season memorable.

As spring of 1999 arrived, I took a wonderful vacation to Budapest, Vienna and Prague, three cities that had been on my list for years. Two years before, on a bus in Bolivia, I sat down next to a tall blonde and we chatted during the trip. When she said she was from Prague, I asked for her phone number and told her that someday I would show up.

The previous year, 1998, on a bus to Victoria Falls in Zimbabwe, I was wearing a shirt from Greece. A guy with an Aussie accent struck up a conversation. When I mentioned that I had coached swimming in Greece, he asked if I knew George Carpuzis. George was a Greek-Canadian coach I had met in Greece and who worked with the Aussie at the American School in Budapest. So, I got his telephone number, too. Then when I bought my ticket, I called both my contacts. The Aussie invited me to stay at his place in Budapest. I did have dinner with George one night. I hadn't seen him in more than 10 years. I also looked up another woman, a Hungarian I had met in Capetown, South Africa in 1996 and she and her boyfriend took me sightseeing.

After almost being killed by a huge bag of laundry thrown from a 4th floor balcony by the maids at my hotel in Vienna, which missed me by about a foot, I took the train to Prague. I met my bus trip acquaintance at a horse stables where she spent time riding. She told me that she was too tall for me but had arranged for me to stay with her girlfriend who was more my size. Luck of the devil, again.

Prague remains one of my favorite cities to this day. It was fortunate not to have been bombed during WWII. The center of the city is a wonderful medieval fairyland of palaces and bridges that transport you to another era.

Before departing on that adventure, I was in the athletic director's office at the HS when the secretary said she had heard I was going on a trip. I was excited as I told her of the wonderful places I would be traveling to. She responded, "Why ever would you want to go there? The best mall is in Peoria." To each his own, I suppose.

Back from Europe, batteries recharged, I began preparing the swimmers for the summer season to culminate at the Illinois State Junior Olympics in Chicago. Meanwhile, my friend Mr. T, ever on the warpath, was temporarily on his own since his lawyer had petitioned the court to be relieved of the case due to Mr. T's incessant calls, emails and faxes, as if the lawyer had no other cases to attend to. Just a few days before the deadline to find another lawyer, he was again successful. Both took the case on contingency because Mr. T was broke.

We had a local bank that was planning to sponsor a large record board for the pool with the HS and club records. Mr. T went to the bank and told them that the club was on the verge of collapsing and not to fund the record board. They withdrew their offer. The club board then voted to cancel Mr. T's family membership. He proceeded to expand his lawsuit to include all the members of the board of the club.

That July, the swimmers had great performances at the Illinois State Junior Olympics, winning three events, including a relay that was 3rd in the national top 16 ranking that year and finishing in 7th place overall in team scoring. Just a week later, disaster struck again. My 13-year-old super talented breaststroker, who had won two golds the previous week, was at the pool with a couple of girl friends, with no lifeguards on duty, late on a Saturday afternoon. The girls were doing underwater swims across the pool. At one point, one of the girls noticed Jenny, the best swimmer of the three, just floating face down, in the water. They pulled her out with the help of a boy. It seems her lungs were full of water so CPR wasn't doing any good. By the time the paramedics arrived, she had suffered permanent brain damage from loss of oxygen. She wasn't expected to survive the night.

Jenny did survive and has made extraordinary progress but she has never walked again. Never was a person less deserving of such a fate. Her mom, dad and brother are about the nicest people you would ever want to meet.

Life does go on and a couple of weeks later, we began my second HS season with the girls, having quite a strong team and high expectations, even without Jenny's presence. I solved the mystery in Quincy of why swimmers often did better during the HS season than the club season: shorter, more exciting meets, more team spirit, HS team pride and accolades from your high school peers.

The days flew by and the girls were getting psyched up. Our goals included winning the conference championships and qualifying at least four girls for the state HS championships. The ever persistent Mr. T was not about to let it happen, though. At some point during the season, he notified the State HS Association that I had been breaking the training rules, coaching the club and HS teams together. That season, we were meticulous in following the rules to avoid any possible violations. Mr. T's allegations were unfounded but his word was accepted without any investigation, and just a week before the conference meet, I was told by my lawyer that I had been suspended by the IHSA and could no longer coach the HS team.

The girls were devastated and I had reached the end of my patience. I went to the school superintendent and asked why the HS didn't ask for an injunction to stay the suspension until a hearing was held and the facts examined. I'll never forget his inane reply: "We don't want to piss them off further."

When I told my lawyer this, he told me to talk to the assistant superintendent who really ran the district. Relating my conversation to the assistant superintendent, he shouted out to his secretary, "Get Joe down here now." Joe denied having made the statement. Later that week, with the swimmers' parents up in arms, including the federal judge, the HS district sent its lawyers to Springfield to try to get the suspension overturned. When they returned, they confidently said that it would all be resolved on the following Monday.

So, on Monday, the ruling came down: my suspension was doubled to two years! The lawyers went back again and this time a compromise was reached. I could resume coaching but I could not accompany the swimmers to the sectional meet that weekend and I would be on probation. At the conference meet the previous Saturday, which I could not attend either, we lost by a narrow margin.

When I asked to see the ruling on my suspension, I was invited to the office of the school district lawyers. What they showed me had been at least 50 percent blacked out. The documents looked like some national security papers. What I later learned was that Quincy HS had been violating the state recruiting rules for its basketball team for years, recruiting Eastern European players illegally. Basketball is the premier sport in downstate Illinois and the only sport anyone cared about. The school cut a deal to save the basketball program from suspension and, in exchange, sold the swim team down the river. Immediately after the HS season ended in mid-November, I notified the club that I was resigning as of the end of the winter season in late February. This would give the club ample time to find another coach. My issue was not with the club.

Just two weeks before the winter state championships, my best swimmer was diagnosed with mono. But, it was not your average case. In line with all the other "happenings" in Quincy, her spleen was on the verge of exploding. It took her close to a year to fully recover. Then, my best male swimmer, who had placed second in the Illinois State meet the previous summer, blew out his knee and he was done for the season. At some point, you just have to laugh in order not to cry.

I got through the meet and began packing, planning to leave in another ten days. I had prepared a trip that would take me around the world, giving clinics in several countries and coaching a team in Zimbabwe for five months. On a Wednesday afternoon ten days before my planned departure, I received a call from the Illinois State Police saying they were notified that I had been abusing a minor and would like to question me. I immediately called my lawyer in Springfield who was hired and paid for by the school district which was responsible for my defense as a school employee for the duration of the case. She later told me the State Police did a six-month examination of my case before dropping it.

The next day, I received a call from some organization that defends abused children telling me they, too, received a call that I had been abusing a minor. My lawyer took care of that, too. Mr. T just never gave up.

On Friday, I got a call from my lawyer: "Next Monday or Tuesday you will receive a subpoena to appear as a witness in Mr. T's case against the school district which is in state court. If you receive the subpoena you must appear." She knew I was leaving shortly and, thankfully, she gave me the heads up.

That night I called my friend, Joe, who was now living in Bettendorf, Iowa and said, "Joe, I need you to help get my ass out of here this weekend." Joe drove down with a van and we packed everything and left the apartment on Sunday. Sure enough, the subpoena was delivered, unsuccessfully, on Monday.

My case was dismissed on three occasions, and reopened twice, on appeal. Eventually, Mr. T also lost his second lawyer but continued to pursue the case on his own. He finally ran out of options and after a total of seven years, I was advised by my lawyer that the case was closed. Mr. T was given the bill for thousands of dollars in court costs, so some justice was served.

I must admit that the Quincy experience pretty much depleted whatever energy I had left for coaching kids. When I embarked on my trip in March 2000, I needed some time to map out my immediate future. Giving clinics is generally enjoyable and relatively stress free and, in addition, it pays the bills on the short term. I have always utilized the clinics to expand my travel horizons, visiting neighboring countries after the clinic since my transportation has already been paid for. I broke up my trip into sections, going first to Brazil, then Southeast Asia, Africa and finally, Brazil again. More on the clinic experiences in a later chapter.

Chapter XVII
Zimbabwe, 2000-2001

I first visited Zimbabwe in 1998, utilizing, as my initial contact, the parents of a diver at Western Illinois University who was from a wealthy white family in Harare. Her parents were really nice people but they lived in their insulated white world in black Africa.

One day, I asked the mom about going to the central market to buy some handicrafts and she offered to take me there. When we arrived and left the car guarded by the driver, she mentioned that her mother had lived her whole life in Zimbabwe/Rhodesia and had never been to that market. It was where the blacks shopped.

From Harare, I was sent on to the second city, Bulawayo and was hosted by a family there, too. The wife, Lorna, was a coach of a club called the Crusaders. It was winter and the water was too cold to swim in so I gave a talk for the local coaches at Lorna's home.

I also went to Victoria Falls, a spectacular place to visit on the Zambezi River, dividing Zimbabwe from Zambia. I had paid a deposit of $50 to reserve a room for three days in a nice hotel near the falls. But when I checked out to pay the balance of my bill, the clerk said everything was in order so I just walked out and got on the plane as fast as I could.

The following year, I contacted Lorna again and told her I would be available to spend a season coaching the swimmers and, aware of their limited resources, I said I would be happy to do it if they would just cover my living expenses. She was able to secure a commitment from the team members and we were in business. They found a woman who had a vacant guest house in her yard and was willing to allow me to stay there. The guest house was very nice but it had a thatched roof from which scorpions occasionally fell to the floor. I was always terrified that I would step on one. They were small but their sting could put you in the hospital for a couple of days. Other parents supplied the house with utensils and linens. I was given a car, the first and only Mercedes I will ever have. The owner of a gas station gave me free gas. Families would often invite me over for dinner and I was given a food allowance, too.

At this point, it is important to discuss the political situation of Zimbabwe at that time and give some historical background. Everyone is familiar with Zimbabwe's despotic dictator Robert Mugabe, who has been in power since 1980, and who has totally destroyed his country. How did this happen?

Leading one of the two main guerilla groups fighting for independence from what was Rhodesia and the white racist government that had declared independence from the British in 1965, Mugabe decided to consolidate his power at the end of the war for liberation by sending his troops to massacre an estimated 20,000 members of the other guerilla army and rival tribe.

In the early years of independence, Zimbabwe flourished economically and was a major exporter of food products and tobacco. Mugabe allowed most of the white landowners to maintain ownership of their large farms which employed thousands of blacks in, by African standards, fairly decent conditions. He paid lip service to the promise of land reform. Of course Mugabe took his cut of the farmers' profits.

In 2000, after years of political oppression, for the first time, polls showed that Mugabe was at risk of losing the election. He needed an issue to galvanize his followers. That issue, land reform, became the death knell of the economy. Mugabe declared that he was going to confiscate the white-owned farms and distribute the land to black farmers. He sent mobs of thugs to drive out the white farmers but, as a consequence, the thousands of black laborers on those farms lost their jobs and had little recourse but to move to the slums in the cities. The supposed beneficiaries of the policy turned out to be mostly Mugabe's political cronies who knew nothing of farming and had no intention of developing the land. So, almost overnight, Zimbabwe went from a bread basket to a basket case. Opposition leaders were beaten and killed and Mugabe succeeded in winning the election by a narrow margin. Most of the whites fled to other countries.

Bulawayo, where I stayed, was the center of the opposition to Mugabe and often suffered for it. When I arrived in November 2000, the white population was less than one percent of the total. On the other hand, about 98 percent of the swimmers were white. Some of the reasons were obvious, the poverty in the black townships, the dearth of swimming pools where the blacks lived and, a contributing factor, the belief among many whites that blacks cannot be good swimmers, anyway, so why waste time trying to teach them.

With the economy in shambles, it was difficult to get the chemicals and parts necessary to keep the pools running. At our municipal 50 meter pool in Bulawayo, the ancient pipes would often break, which forced the manager to shut down the filter system while they tried to fix the problem. The water would gradually change color from blue to green to black, and we would borrow another pool until ours was reopened.

At our first local swim meet, I was appalled to find that the judges, timers and parents around the pool were smoking. I really pissed people off when I told them not to smoke. Another shocking revelation was the ingrained racism of the whites. I mentioned that many families invited me to dinner. The conversation invariably led to disparaging remarks about the bloody *kafirs* (niggers) and other comments that sounded just like the racist attitudes of southern whites towards the blacks in the US back in the 50s.

I lived about 10 kilometers from the city. When I went downtown to shop or see a movie, I was often the only white person in sight. I always greeted people with a smile and said hi. My accent gave me away; the blacks knew immediately that I was not local. When asked, I would say I was from the US and their faces would light up. No ugly American image there. My being from the US really broke the ice. Everyone was very friendly to me. One time I got a lift back to Harare from a black father of one of the swimmers from a small team in a little town where I had spent a week giving a clinic. He was so grateful to be able to chat freely with someone about the horrible repression in his country that he never stopped talking during the three-hour ride.

One evening at a restaurant, I met Zimbabwe's leading author, whose books have been reviewed favorably in the *New York Times*. She was sitting at the next table and we struck up a conversation. I asked her out and we went for a drive the next day to a wonderful game park near Bulawayo. On the way, we were stopped at a police checkpoint. I was pulled aside and she was questioned by two police officers. Finally released, she told me that they were suspicious of her because she was traveling with a white guy. Fortunately, her fame and status in the country were enough to secure our release.

I was able to get a pass to visit the game parks as if I were Zimbabwean rather than a foreigner. Instead of paying $10 to $25 to enter the parks, I paid pennies. I took total advantage of it and often spent the day bird watching or just driving through the parks gazing at the fascinating animals and scenic rock formations.

The only time I felt animosity from a black person was one day when I was out jogging in a smaller town. Across the street, a tall young black man called out to me in an aggressive tone "Hey, you are short and you are old." I replied with a smile, "Hey, you got that right," and went on my merry way. Many of the blacks would take an English word they liked and use it to name one of their children. Names like Justice and Freedom were not uncommon but my favorite was a guy I met in Bulawayo whose real name was "Whatever."

I went to Victoria Falls again and signed up for a kayak trip on the Zambezi River. Arriving at the tour office, I was assigned a "kayak" which was really a rectangular rubber raft for two. My crew mate was a young, powerful-looking guy from Chicago who was there with some friends. We started off ok but at one place, we came too close to a herd of hippos, Africa's most lethal animal to humans. They are very territorial and will go underwater, overturn your boat, and chomp you with their powerful jaws. I was steering our kayak when the guide yelled to hurry up and get away from the hippos. I harassed my partner to speed it up but he was of little help. I couldn't believe this strong guy was such a wimp. We did get away safely, though. The next day I went to meet his group for dinner and found out that he was in the hospital with malaria. I really felt bad about how I had chewed him out the previous day.

The trip back to Bulawayo from Victoria Falls on the beautiful Leopard bus was about a seven-hour drive. When I arrived at the departure point, the bus was nowhere to be seen. I waited a while until I finally asked a guy at the bus stop. He said the trip had been cancelled but I could take the Zebra bus, which was not quite as comfy. I waited for the Zebra for another half hour before being told that it was also cancelled. What to do?

At that point, another guy said, "You better get on the bus over there." I looked to where he pointed and saw a rusted wreck with shattered windows. When I got on I had to climb over the mounds of baggage piled up in the aisle to work my way back to a seat almost in the rear. Next to me was a woman nursing two babies. I asked her how long the ride was and found out that I was looking at 10 hours, minimum. Why ten hours? One contributing factor was that the driver would stop at roadside taverns periodically for a cold one but the passengers had to stay on the bus. I was the only white person on the bus and everyone was friendly enough but I had nothing to eat or drink for the duration and couldn't get off, even to pee. For someone with an enlarged prostate, it was an achievement to have survived that trip.

I accompanied the swimmers to the capital, Harare, for the combined age group and senior nationals. The meet was held in a world class facility built five years before for the All Africa Championships. The pool was cleaned once a year for the meet and left to rot the rest of the time, being located in the heart of the black township area where no one ever swam. Once again, timers, judges, coaches and parents were smoking on deck and in the swimmers' waiting areas, ironically, often just below the non-smoking signs.

I was invited to give a talk between prelims and finals one day for the coaches and parents. Once again, I cited the FINA rule prohibiting smoking at meet venues but I was told to mind my own business. I antagonized everyone further when I pointed out that out of 128 participants at the meet, only four were black. I stressed that if there was to be any hope for competitive swimming in the country, someone would have to begin training young black coaches and start lesson programs for the black kids, too.

One of the coaches made the standard comment that everyone knows blacks can't be good swimmers, so why bother. The future Olympic Champion, Kirsty Coventry was at the meet and she had just received a scholarship offer from Auburn University. Her coach, who had never heard of Auburn, asked me if it was a good place and I said, yes, it would be an excellent choice. As they say, the rest is history.

Before departing Quincy for another overseas adventure, I knew I had to catch up with the modern world if I wanted to stay in touch with friends while moving from country to country. I asked one of my 15-year old kids to teach me the basics on her computer, acquired an email address and bought a laptop. When I arrived in Zimbabwe in November of 2000, I began checking the ASCA job service website to see what was available.

Over the previous couple of years, I had given some clinics for masters swim teams and found them to be more fun and rewarding than the standard clinics for coaches and kids. The adult swimmers were so appreciative of the help they received at the clinics, plus, you could talk to them about anything without having to worry about the liability consequences and even enjoy a beer with them after the session. I found an ad for the Davis Aquatic Masters (DAM) and applied.

Chapter XVIII
Davis Aquatic Masters, Davis, California, Sweet and Sour, 2001-08

DAM, the first of the so called mega masters teams in the US, had been founded some 25 years before by the world famous tri athlete, Dave Scott. At the time I applied, the club was going through a minor crisis. Membership had dropped while looking for a new coach, with an interim coach holding things together in the meantime. I was chosen for an interview and flown to California after returning from Zimbabwe. Following a luncheon with several members and the formal interview, there was a party in the evening at the club president's home. I had brought with me a couple of bottles of *cachaca*, a Brazilian liquor, and proceeded to introduce those present to *caipirinhas*, the national drink of Brazil. Some say I was hired because of my bartending skills. One of the people who interviewed me, Scott Harris, coincidentally, was the son of a college coach I had known back in Illinois. I'm sure that connection didn't hurt, either.

During the interview, I asked the president what percentage of the swimmers actually attended meets. After a short silence, he responded, "About 10 percent." I was shocked and wondered if I was in the right place. In my previous contacts with masters programs, they had all been highly competitive groups. In fact, they all had a competition requirement as a component of the membership process. The competitive aspect of coaching had been such an important aspect of the job to me for the previous 35 years that I just took it for granted. But coaches always feel they can make dramatic changes in a program and I was confident that I would soon have lots of swimmers competing.

There are positives and negatives in coaching masters. On the positive side, coaching masters swimmers meant that I no longer needed to deal with pushy parents of age-group swimmers, nor would there be the stress related to producing results from your swimmers in meets. In addition, the frustrations and disappointments associated with the politics of international swimming would not be a factor. The social aspect of masters swimming is very important to many of the members and quite enjoyable for the coach, as well. The dinners, parties, going to movies and shows were all great fun and filled my life in Davis. The fact that most swimmers swam for fitness and health rather than meet results allowed me to travel more often, taking full advantage of my vacation days and continuing to give clinics each year around the world.

On the flip side, I would miss the high that comes with the great performances my swimmers attained at taper meets after training devotedly all season to reach a goal. It is not unusual for masters swimmers to think they know more than the coach and to let him know it. You cannot expect masters swimmers to be on time or to stay to the end of practice. In spite of trying everything I could think of, I was not really able to make a dent in the non-competitive philosophy of the club members. Most masters swimmers only train two to three times a week, so real improvement is limited anyway.

Satisfaction for the coach comes in other ways, most often from seeing your swimmers improve their technique, learn a new stroke or turn, and sometimes from sharing their sense of achievement and pleasure after swimming a personal best at a meet. We did have several former college swimmers who were able to achieve personal best times, though they only trained one hour a day, five to six days a week compared to the 15-20 hours of training they had done during their college days. That, too, was gratifying.

While in Davis, I celebrated my 60th birthday. One of my swimmers, Betty Dugan, had a party at her house where I was given the best birthday present I have ever received. Betty had come up with the idea of a calendar, with the photos of 12 of my lovely swimmers, ranging in age from 25 to 75, one page for each month, all topless but covered by some item, for example a turkey for November with the Thanksgiving theme. It is a gift I will always treasure.

Soon after I arrived in Davis, I thought, what a wonderful opportunity I now had to share some of the beautiful spots I had visited around the world with my current swimmers. Another advantage of masters is that you don't need permission from their parents for the swimmers to travel. You don't have to fund raise, either. You make the proposal to the group and those who have the time, interest and financial ability sign up. To justify the trip as a swimming trip, I would call on my friends overseas to commit to organizing a meet for us. Sometimes it was put together hastily and without much organization, but on other occasions, we participated in highly competitive meets.

Our first trip was to Brazil, my favorite overseas destination. Unfortunately, the payment deadline was soon after the 9/11 disaster and many people were hesitant to fly in those uncertain times. I was only able to convince 16 brave souls to join. My former club, A Hebraica of Sao Paulo, organized an excellent invitational meet. Our itinerary included a trip to Iguacu falls, the most amazing waterfalls in the world, where we took rubber motorized boats right under the falls.

In Sao Paulo, two club members offered their beachfront apartments in Guaruja, the beach town, only 45 minutes from Sao Paulo where the Paulistas head on weekends, swelling the population from 200,000 to two million. We went during the week and had the beach to ourselves. As the swimmers raced to the warm water, I noticed a guy with a wooden pushcart selling my favorite drink, *caipirinhas*. A simple delicious drink made of limes, sugar, ice and the *cachaca* liquor or vodka, there is nothing more refreshing on a hot day. I ordered one, a triple shot, for $1. It was excellent and I ran to the shore line to pass it around to the swimmers. In no time, they had consumed enough to put the average person out of commission. It was a struggle to get back across the street to our apartments. I had a hangover the next day for the first time in 20 years.

The vendor became our instant buddy who followed us around on the beach for the next two days.

The following year, we went to my second favorite travel destination, Greece. That trip included meets in Athens and Hania, the Acropolis tourist trap and a wonderful visit to the island of Santorini, which in my opinion, is the most beautiful island in the Mediterranean. A couple of days before leaving Santorini for Crete I went to purchase our tickets and was told that our ship had been cancelled. I tried to book another but was informed it was a national holiday and all agencies were closed.

The following day, I went again to the booking office and was able to get us on a hovercraft at just about the same price and half the travel time. We arrived at the port of Heraklion on the other end of Crete and looked for our bus to take us to Hania. When I was unable to locate it, I called the club in Hania and was told the bus broke down on the way but should be arriving soon. Then, walking through the parking lot, I saw our bus sitting there. I went into a restaurant next to the lot and found the driver. He wolfed down the rest of his meal and we were on our way. About half way to Hania he checked in with his office and was told to take us back. The club had switched bus companies but never told me. I insisted he continue and we ended up paying his company and not the other.

Most of the swimmers hiked down the 15 kilometer Samaria Gorge, beginning at about 7,000 feet and ending at a small town on the southern coast of Crete. It is a wonderful hike with the scenery changing constantly but I had left the hospital just five weeks before after a quadruple bypass and was unable to accompany them. We also spent three days on a secluded beach on the south side of Crete called Sougia, a place I never miss on my numerous trips to Crete. Finally, we returned to Athens to spend a short night at a hotel before our early morning departure for the US.

Arriving at the airport after the ferry boat ride from Crete, we discovered that the taxi drivers had gone on strike that day. Luckily, I found a city bus that would take us from the airport, dropping us just in front of our hotel. We piled on along with another 30 to 40 upset passengers. Yes, the bus dropped us by our hotel but on the wrong side of a major highway, with three lanes in each direction and non-stop traffic. I had no idea how we were going to reach the other side. We had an 80-year old with us who didn't walk that well, either. Once again, with a touch of my unique brand of divine intervention, the traffic literally disappeared on both sides of the street for just long enough for us to cross over. I now know how Moses must have felt when the waters parted.

In 2004, we returned to Brazil again. This time, we stopped in Rio de Janeiro for a couple of days and visited the major tourist sites including Sugar Loaf and the Christ Statue at night. Departing Rio to head north, our guide took us to the wrong airport. So, at 7 AM, we tried to check in at the international airport, one hour from the city, only to be told our flight was leaving from the domestic airport located right across the street from the hotel we had just left. The guide was able to recall our bus and called his boss, who somehow convinced the airline to hold the plane for us. When we arrived at the correct airport, we were ushered right to the tarmac, without any security checks and rushed to our plane. It was almost like being celebrities.

We flew to San Luis, an old colonial city in the north, visited the wonderful sand dunes and lagoons called the Sheets of Maranhao, toured the colonial areas of the city and Alcantara, where the rich planters had homes during the colonial period, and trained at a local club. Heading back south, we stopped at Recife for an invitational swim meet, competing in pouring rain for two days. In Recife, we visited some of the famous beaches north of the city, its sister city Olinda, a charming old colonial town, as well as the market place, to stock up on souvenirs. We couldn't swim at the beach across the street from the hotel because the city beaches were all closed due to a recent spate of shark attacks.

Our last stop on that trip was in Juez de Fora, a very forgettable city, to compete in the national masters championship meet. The pool was old and inadequate for a meet but the atmosphere was fun. Once the swimmers were in the water to begin a race, the samba music would blast out and swimmers danced on deck while the competitors raced.

The following year, we went to Portugal, one of my favorite European destinations. That trip began with a couple of days at the beach on the Algarve, then a bus trip back to Lisbon with the world's rudest bus driver. In Lisbon, we toured the city for three wonderful days. From the old forts and monasteries to the beautiful new aquarium, and from delicious pastels to port wine, Lisbon has it all. A stopover in the old university city of Coimbra was great and then, on to Anadia, a lovely town in the wine country where we had our swimming competition.

Our hosts planned it well. With swimmers from Spain competing, in addition to the Portuguese, it was a nice mix of friendly people. Three wineries sponsored the meet. The daily schedule was, compete in the morning and visit the wineries in the afternoon. Instead of medals, bottles of wine and champagne were awarded, just perfect for masters swimmers. We were well supplied for the next four days' happy hours.

Following the competition, the mayor hosted a lunch on the balcony of the wine museum. As we sat around the beautifully arranged tables, we heard bagpipes in the distance. Winding through the orchard below the balcony was a group of musicians playing their bagpipes and dressed in monks' robes. They joined us at our table and played again after dinner, as the swimmers danced to the wonderful music. We finished off that trip with a visit to the exquisite medieval walled town of Evora, a fitting finale to what many said was our best trip to date.

In 2007, we returned to Greece but with some variations in the itinerary. A one-day stop at the tiny island of Hydra kicked off the trip. We hiked up to the monastery overlooking the harbor in 100 degree heat. It was a killer. Returning on an afternoon hovercraft to Athens, we grabbed our bags at the hotel and had to rush to connect with the overnight ferry to Crete. We had the usual swim meet and open water swim in Hania, the hike down the Samaria Gorge and a couple days again in Sougia for beach time and happy hours.

The last leg of the trip, following the ferry ride back to Athens involved a mad rush to connect with the ferry to the island of Milos. I'm sure we amused the bystanders. We were 30 people pulling suitcases, running along the harbor to the next boat. We barely made it in time. Milos is another favorite of mine. Relatively off the beaten path and with great photos waiting to be taken at every turn, it has nice beaches, great sunsets from the chapel at the top of the island, excellent restaurants and a more laid-back atmosphere than the better known islands.

The final trip before I left Davis was very satisfying, personally, because it was to Ecuador, my very first country overseas. I realized a long-time dream of mine which was to someday return with my team to compete there. The inclusion of the Galapagos Islands in our itinerary made it the most popular trip of all. Seventy people signed up, double the number from any previous trip. I was a bit apprehensive about a group that large but they were amazing and got along like family—better than family, actually. The Islands are an expensive destination but I discovered that it doesn't have to be. Instead of touring the islands by live-in boat, we stayed in the main town and took small boats daily to island hop. It cut the expenses in half.

My Ecuadorian friends organized a competition at the same pool where I had worked as a Peace Corps volunteer 40 years earlier. After the meet, we boarded a bus to go to the dinner and awards ceremony. Our driver got confused and missed the turnoff. He then backed up for a mile on a major highway at dusk, one of the scariest rides I have ever taken, so he could make the turn-off, rather than go around again.

I got the chance to visit with many old friends on that trip. Before the meet in Guayaquil, we took a day trip to Salinas, a major beach resort, toured Guayaquil, tried their famously delicious roast pork sandwiches and enjoyed the riverfront promenade and night life.

Flying to the Galapagos, we were met by our lovely hostess, Esther Fuentes, who owned the hotel most of us stayed in, and had arranged our housing, the daily boat trips, guides and scuba diving for our divers. We had an open water swim in the bay at Puerto Ayora, the main town, which was challenging, amid the waves and numerous jellyfish. Our daily trips included hikes, visits to the Darwin center and to several turtle farms where the decimated turtle population is being replenished. Excellent snorkeling opportunities were part of the daily plan as well.

After the Galapagos, the final leg, Quito, provided quite a contrast. A dramatically beautiful drive through the Andes included stops at the Equator monument and a bird restoration park where injured hawks, owls and even the magnificent Andes Condor were on display, and concluded at Otavalo, a large native Indian town with the most famous handicraft market in South America. Everyone stocked up on colorful souvenirs at the market. I think the buses doubled in weight on the return to Quito. The next day, we took the tour of Colonial Quito and finally welcomed a free day for more shopping and visits to the local museums. It was my swan song at Davis Aquatic Masters.

DAM is the largest adult swim team in the world with over 600 members annually. With those numbers, we ran nine daily workouts to accommodate our swimmers. My contract required 20 to 25 hours a week of on-deck coaching which left me with another 20+ hours to cover with assistant coaches. Finding competent coaches to help me was probably the most frustrating aspect of the job.

Initially, I tried to cover the hours with a group of seven to eight often unreliable college students. When I could see that wasn't working, I advertised for an assistant. My first two assistants were more work than I had bargained for. One, very enthusiastic and energetic to begin with, never finished an assignment and eventually began to undermine my authority, badmouthing me to the swimmers, undoubtedly hoping to get me fired so he could take over the head coach position. The same pattern was repeated in that person's next coaching job. My other assistant was under the impression that masters coaching was the same as college coaching, and spent as much time as possible with the fast swimmers, despite repeated warnings, and ignored the majority who were just fitness swimmers.

Finally, when that coach began sending religious messages to the male swimmers, he was asked to leave. But, third time is a charm and my next assistant coach, Craig Keller, a young man doing graduate work at the university, was all I could have hoped for and more than made up for the other two. Craig was not only enthusiastic and energetic but also knowledgeable and responsible. We had an excellent working relationship that made my last year and a half at the club much more fun.

After seven years at the helm of the club, a new board of directors took office in January 2008. The incoming president made it clear from the start that her mission was to change head coaches and proceeded to make my life miserable by micromanaging everything. The weak-kneed members of the board either acquiesced or didn't have the courage to stand up to her.

One morning, I woke up and said to myself, "I really don't need to deal with this shit. Why not retire and write a book?" And so I did.

On the lighter side, I became the only one of the five long-term DAM head coaches not to succumb to my swimmers' charms and was able to maintain my bachelor status to the end. The other four head coaches all married one of their swimmers. One incident definitely helped me keep my nose clean. I was going out with one of the swimmers sporadically and one day she walked into the pool while I was coaching and blurted out, "Where have you been? I have my needs, too." It was rather embarrassing, to say the least.

I had been thinking for some time about my options for retirement. I checked out Puerto Rico but didn't like it. I looked into Crete, but couldn't imagine, after living in California, remaining in a place with lots of smokers and without a library with English language books in it. And, so, I eventually narrowed my choices down to Brazil and the Philippines. With the high incidence of street violence in its cities and the rising cost of living in Brazil, I decided on the Philippines.

I contacted a couple of my buddies who are active in swimming and had set up clinics for me in the past and asked for advice. Mark Joseph, the current president of the Swimming Federation, told me to forget retirement, that I would work for his organization, giving clinics, training coaches, directing swim camps, etc. This is exactly the type of work I enjoy, without the full-time commitment to coaching. I have found that after an eight-year hiatus, working with kids is fun again and really much more rewarding than coaching masters and getting second guessed all the time. Sometimes we need a change to appreciate what we had. Coaching on a short-term basis with clinics and swim camps is, though, a whole lot different than the day-to-day coaching gig.

Chapter XIX
Coaching Clinics in 30 Countries, Traveling in 68, 1974-Present

As the reader may have gleaned, much of my travels have been job related, having coached in 10 different countries. In 1974, I received an invitation from a swim team in the town of Piracicaba, in Sao Paulo state, Brazil, to give talks to swimmers and coaches about the success of my teams and general coaching topics. I was so nervous at that first clinic but once I started, I discovered that it was fun sharing my knowledge and the audience was usually receptive. Soon, I realized I could promote the clinics as a way to see more of the world. All sorts of unexpected things happened at the clinics.

On two occasions, I was cheated by the clinic hosts, once in Paraguay, the other time in Brazil. Both times I was dropped off at the airport and told, "Sorry, we don't have the money, good-bye." I was furious but there wasn't anything I could do about it.

Also in Brazil, years later, I was giving a clinic in Curitiba and enjoying lunch at a former swimmers house between sessions. Suddenly, from the TV in the next room I heard someone with a horrible American accent being interviewed. I had always prided myself on my excellent Portuguese. I said to my friend, "What a terrible accent that guy has." She replied, "That is you, you idiot. That's the interview you gave yesterday." How embarrassing!

On another occasion, hired by a private club in Bangkok, the club's coach left on vacation the day I began and only returned after I had left. He wanted to show everyone that he already knew it all and didn't need an American coach to tell him what to do.

At my former club in Hania, Crete, before my talk for the swimmers, the coach called them together and told them not to pay attention to what I said. In Bali, for another clinic, the translator failed to appear. Each day the students would show up and we would wait for an hour before heading for the beach. That was a great paid vacation.

Through my Filipino friend, Ral Rosario, I was able to travel to many areas of his country to give clinics on my numerous trips to that land of 7,000 islands, volcanoes, wonderful dive sites and great food. Because of recurring political problems, including a decades-old communist insurgency and a Muslim separatist rebellion in the southernmost islands, as well as government corruption and mismanagement, the Philippines has not developed its tourist infrastructure to the level of other Southeast Asian countries. It is a wonderful and inexpensive destination and one of my favorite countries to visit.

Some of my clinics there were unusual. On one occasion in Northern Luzon, the main island, I traveled for 10 hours on a bus through a hurricane to reach my destination. The next day, when I went to the pool to begin the clinic, I was greeted at the pool entrance by a huge banner that read, "High Level Coaching Clinic with American Coach Rick Powers." There were about 50 people in the stands waiting for me.

To get an idea of the level of the participants, I always ask a few questions about their swimming background. How many of you are swim coaches? No hands went up. How many are swimming instructors? Again, not a single hand lifted. How many were competitive swimmers. Still, no response.

"OK, what are you guys doing here?"

One woman, obviously very embarrassed, said that the state governor had ordered all the high schools to send one person to the clinic. None of them ever did or ever planned to work in swimming but were randomly chosen and had no choice but to attend. I spent the week teaching them how to swim. They were very grateful and had a nice vacation at government expense.

Another time, Ral and I went to the lovely island of Palawan for a clinic in a small town in the north. It turned out that there was no swimming pool there. The children trained in the harbor near the pier where the boats docked, moving quickly to avoid the boats and not being able to put their feet on the bottom because it was covered with poisonous sea urchins. Not exactly ideal conditions, but some of the kids were pretty good swimmers.

On another trip, to the southern city of Zamboanga with its large Muslim population, Ral and I were snorkeling off of a small island just one kilometer from the city. Suddenly, a large black cloud rose above the city. We rushed to our boat to return and find out what had happened. A Muslim terrorist had thrown a grenade into a bus at the market place, killing four people and wounding 16 others.

On my first visit to the Philippines, one of Ral's brothers took me with him and some friends, including a town mayor to a very nice beach resort called Puerto Galera. The mayor would send his body guards to pick magic mushrooms in the morning and have the resort cook mix them in our omelets for breakfast. At Puerto Galera, the coral reefs were the most colorful I had ever seen. I wonder why.

I gave clinics on two occasions in Bombay (Mumbai), India. I met an Indian coach at a clinic in the US one year and got his address. He was a super guy but, tragically, he died of a brain hemorrhage while visiting the US in 2001, just days after 9/11. After the clinics, I would spend two to three weeks traveling around that incredible country, each time choosing a different region. India is one of those places where you must have infinite patience because anything that can go wrong will go wrong. But you will see some of the most beautiful sights in the world, starting with the Taj Mahal and continuing on to a myriad of palaces and fortresses that dwarf Europe's finest.

On one trip, of six domestic flights, two were cancelled and the others delayed by three to six hours. After one of the cancellations, the airline put me and my girlfriend, Mary in a taxi to our next destination. It was a nine-hour taxi ride at night. In India at that time, virtually all the trucks on the highway had no tail lights and emitted very black exhaust. I couldn't watch. It was so scary. Suddenly, the taxi would overtake a truck that just appeared out of nowhere. We had so many near misses. Seeing carcasses of smashed buses, trucks and cars by the side of the highway didn't build much confidence, either.

Trying to change money one day in Jaipur, we asked the hotel manager which bank would be best. Arriving at the bank, we were told that they only changed traveler's checks. Three banks later, Mary decided to use her credit card to get some cash. The bank manager said he would send a telex to her bank in Singapore to confirm if she had money in her account. We waited for half an hour. Another couple who came in trying to change their dollars was also sent packing. The woman began to cry but I burst out laughing at the absurdity of the situation. Hearing my laughter, the bank manager came running, shouting, "No laughing permitted in my bank," and threw us out.

We then went back to the hotel where the receptionist looked at his watch and told me to run to the local branch of the Bank of India, two blocks away which was closing in ten minutes, and maybe I would get lucky. I arrived at the bank with five minutes to spare, walked up to the counter and gave the woman my passport and a $100 bill. She pointed to another desk where a guy was counting some papers. I sat down in front of him with my passport and money in my hand. He never looked up.

After a minute, I asked "Change money?" No response whatsoever.

Again, I asked, but a bit louder. I figured he was hard of hearing, so I jumped over the desk shoved my passport and money in his face and shouted, "Is this a fucking bank?"

He never batted an eye. I got up, walked out the door and slammed it as hard as I could. As I descended the steps in a rage, a short Indian man who was walking up, shrugged his shoulders and said to me, "This is India." I needed the reminder.

Out of options, we ended up changing our money at the hotel at a very unfavorable rate. On other occasions at banks, when the teller would give me the rupees and I would count them, there was often a discrepancy. I would say "This isn't correct." And he would bring out exactly what was missing from under the counter. Undoubtedly, some foreigners didn't count the amount and the teller would keep part of it for himself.

Mary and I did a city tour in Jodhpur one day. The tour took us to a white hut where several village elders were sitting around smoking opium. We declined their invitation. The guide told us that in the backward areas, the elders would tell the locals which candidate to vote for in the elections. India is known throughout the world for its endemic corruption.

At the Asian Championships in 1988, I met an Indian swimmer, the only one to ever win a medal at the Asian Championships. His reward was a post as deputy superintendent of a police district in New Delhi. When I visited Delhi in 1994, I decided to look him up. He was still something of a national hero so when I mentioned his name to the hotel receptionist, she was able to locate him for me. He was now the superintendent.

I called him and he said he would come over to see me the next evening. I waited but he never showed. The following day, I called again and he promised to meet me that evening at the home of the *Washington Post* bureau chief where I was now staying. Again, he failed to show. But he finally appeared the next evening, two hours late. When I opened the door, it was immediately obvious that he was high on drugs, probably coke. He could not even stand still and was babbling out of control. He left after five minutes. So much for India's finest.

One year, at a swim meet in Chicago with my Alaskan team, I met two Brazilian coaches, got their names, and a year later, I gave a clinic at one of the coaches' clubs in a small city in the middle of nowhere, Araguaina. Flying to the city on a clear day, my flight was unable to land because of a thick layer of smoke from the burning forests of the Amazon. We had to land in a city 200 miles away and then take a bus. During the bus ride, all you could see on both sides of the highway were burnt-out forests. Local landowners illegally burn the forests, and then use the land for cattle grazing. I was told that for an area the size of France, there were only a dozen federal police assigned to protect the forests. Most of the police are bribed by the landowners to ignore the violations anyway. Environmentalists trying to save the forests are often murdered.

At the clinic, there was a team from a place called Carajas, a town in the middle of the Amazon that has the largest iron ore mine in the world. The town itself is like an American suburb, all laid out with nice homes, schools and a shopping district for the executives who work there. I was invited to visit by their coach and hitched a ride on the team bus. The driver took a shortcut that supposedly would save us four hours from the regular trip. But his information was faulty and at one point we came to a halt where the road construction ended, in the middle of the rain forest. With 30 upset kids on the bus, we had to backup for a mile on the dirt road until we found a place to turn around. It took us 16 hours to arrive at the camp.

I was able to tour the mine and it certainly was an impressive place. The Japanese who funded much of the construction had also built a railroad through the jungle, all the way to the coast, from where the ore was shipped to Japan. I was told there was enough ore for the next 400 years at that site. They had monster trucks that could carry 240 tons each. One of the coolest things there was a zoo that, though fenced, was built right in the jungle.

I have been to both ends of North Africa, Egypt and Morocco. The only other country in North Africa that interested me was Tunisia, which is sandwiched between Libya with its nutty dictator Khadafi, and Algeria with its never ending radical Muslim insurrection. In the early 90s, I telephoned the Tunisian Embassy in Washington DC and while chatting with a staff member, discovered that he had connections with the swimming community in Tunisia. He gave me a couple of names and told me that I would be taken care of there and he would see to it that the local people in Tunis, the largest city, organized a coaching clinic.

As it turned out, the coach who picked me up didn't speak English. On the first day of the clinic, there was no translator and the coaches in attendance didn't pay any attention to what I tried to convey. The second day, the woman translator showed up an hour late by which time, most of the participants had left. On the final day, the translator did arrive on time but none of the coaches came.

As in many cases, the clinic was just an excuse to get me to the country for the cultural and travel experience. Following the clinic, I visited the fascinating *souk* in Tunis, the ruins of Carthage, an interesting small town, Jerba, and signed up for a three-day trip to the Sahara desert. That was the highlight of my trip. We stopped off at a Berber village, Chenini, where the homes are built into the cliffs, and another village, Matmata, which appears in the first Star Wars movie. All the homes are in large pits dug out of the ground. A ramp descends to the bottom and the individual rooms are dug into the walls of the pit, all open to the main courtyard. The only way you can tell you are approaching a house is by the TV antenna sticking up from the hole.

We also visited an oasis and stayed the night in Bedouin tents. The generator at the oasis only functioned for three hours. As we were having dinner under the palm trees at dusk, I happened to glance up and was astounded to see the Milky Way through the palm fronds in such clarity that I had to get closer. After dinner, I talked to the only two other people in the group who spoke English and convinced them to walk out into the desert. We grabbed our sheets from the tents and went about 100 yards to the dunes. There was not a single electric light for a hundred miles. We lay on our backs for hours watching the shooting stars. I have never seen a more brilliant sky, neither on the sea nor in the mountains.

On the down side, during the daytime, you are covered with flies in the desert. They disappear at night and don't seem to bother you if you are dressed in dark blue clothing. There is garbage everywhere in Tunisia, on the roadsides, city streets, even in the desert. The food is very boring with little variety, mostly just shish kabobs and roast chicken. Women do not generally dress in traditional clothing, though they all disappear from the streets at night. Virtually all the men smoke but I never saw a woman smoking. All in all, Tunisia is a good place to get a taste of North African culture. It is safe and peaceful and people are generally quite friendly.

I was sitting at home in Anchorage one day in 1990 when I found a documentary about Vietnam on a cable channel. The Vietnam War had an inadvertent but powerful influence on my life because it pushed me to join the Peace Corps and sent me down an entirely different path, coaching swimming. The documentary was fascinating and I soon bought a ticket to visit that small country that had changed so many Americans lives.

I arrived in Hanoi in 1991 during the period of the US embargo. The craters from the B52 bombings were still evident near the airport. Changing $100 at the bank, I was handed a paper bag full of cash. I couldn't believe it. The 1,100,000 dong lasted me more than two weeks.

My first thought was to try and organize a swim clinic. I took a pedicab to the Sports Ministry and walked down the halls trying, unsuccessfully to find someone who spoke English. When I walked into an office where a woman was sitting behind a desk, I saw on the wall a framed certificate from Cuba. In Spanish, I asked if she had been to Cuba. Her face lit up, "For seven years," she replied.

She locked up the office and spent the day taking me sightseeing. In addition, she called some sports people in Saigon and tried to organize a clinic for me there, while warning me that the people in the south still hated the northerners and probably wouldn't organize anything out of spite.

From Hanoi, I flew to Hue, the former capital, and site of some of the fiercest fighting during the Tet Offensive during the Vietnam War. Most of the city was restored, though work continued on the Forbidden City, the ancient site of the palaces of the Vietnamese royal family. The tombs of the former kings in an area outside the city limits, are well worth the trip.

On my first night in Hue, I was strolling down a street and said hi to three girls walking towards me. With just a few words of English among them, they invited me for an ice cream and told me they were students at the local university. They took me to their dorm and proudly showed me their room. Twelve women slept in one room on four triple-deck bunk beds with no bedding whatsoever, just wooden boards. The next day, the students showed up at my hotel with an extra bicycle and guided me to all the temples, the market place and the Citadel where the North Vietnamese soldiers held out the longest after the American counterattack during Tet.

Everywhere I went, people asked where I was from. When I said, "The US," they would always respond, "America Number One."

One day, I asked a guy, "Why not Russia Number One? They helped you defeat us."

He replied, "Russia, no money. America, much money."

Next, I took a train to Danang, the former American air base, once the busiest airport in the world. I was shown to a seat in a car where all foreigners had to sit together. I was seated next to a French guy who was talking to a Buddhist monk in French. I began to chat with the Frenchman who spoke decent English. When he went to the bathroom, I turned to the monk and asked if he, too, spoke English. He said yes and I asked how long he had been a monk. He leaned closer and said, "I'm no fucking monk. I've been using the robes since the war to get free food, housing and transportation." Another revelation.

I ended up traveling with the Frenchman for a couple of days. We went to a town near Danang which was settled by the Dutch in the 16th century. At a beautiful Chinese temple, I spoke with the caretaker. His family had been caretakers of that temple for 700 years! At one point in the conversation, after admitting that he had spent several years in prison after the war because he had worked for the US, he asked, "Do you want to know why we loved you Americans?"

I said, "Sure, go for it."

"Because it was so easy to steal from you."

I thought of all the young Americans who died for people like him and the corrupt government he represented.

I left Danang and took a taxi to China Beach, a world class beach where the troops went for in-country R & R. It was truly one of the nicest white sand beaches in the world and it was just in the shadow of Marble Mountain, which was a Viet Cong hospital. During the war, there was an unwritten rule among combatants not to shoot at one other, though the soldiers were in close proximity. I was followed around both places by an army of little kids who spoke the most amazing English and just wanted to practice with me.

I was standing in front of the Danang airport awaiting my flight to Saigon when five brand new SUVs pulled up and disgorged a group of what were obviously American soldiers in civilian dress. Surprised, I walked up to two of them and asked what they were doing there. One replied, "Classified information, can't tell you."

I almost laughed. I tried another guy who was standing alone and he admitted they were part of a mission, looking for US prisoners who were missing in action (MIA). I couldn't believe it and walked into the departure lounge shaking my head where I saw two New Zealanders with TV cameras sitting on one of the benches. I went over and said, "You won't believe it but there is a whole platoon of American soldiers outside looking for prisoners of war."

They rushed out and began filming and questioning the soldiers. Meantime, my flight was called early and I had to run to get on the plane as they were closing the door. All the passengers' luggage was piled on vacant seats with no restraints. I just hoped there wouldn't be any turbulence because everything would have flown around. Landing in Saigon, I took a taxi to my hotel, dropped off my stuff and just strolled on the streets, passing the old US Embassy building and other familiar sights from the war period.

I was in the War Museum when a very beautiful young lady approached and asked if she might accompany me so that she could practice her English. She was an English student at one of the universities. We spent the day touring the city on her motorbike and that evening, she brought me to her home for dinner.

Her father was one of the leading painters in Vietnam who was sent to the south after the war along with 200,000 other bureaucrats from the victorious north to take over the administration of the southern provinces. He lamented the restrictive atmosphere for artistic development under the communists since 1956 in the north and brought me to his bedroom where he had a closet full of exquisite paintings that he was never able to show publicly, since he had been limited to doing traditional patriotic murals mandated by the government.

The next day, I found, or more correctly, I was found by a guide with a small motorcycle who brought me to the famous tunnels of Cu Chi where thousands of Viet Cong soldiers hid from the American soldiers and bombing raids. The tunnel system, more than 250 kilometers long and in some places three levels deep, was impressive. It included hospitals and living quarters underground. One section had been widened for the larger western tourists but it was still claustrophobic crawling through. We also drove through an area that had been sprayed with Agent Orange and was still almost bare of vegetation two decades after. It was a sobering experience. I have American friends who were subjected to the effects of the spraying and have suffered severely, but the US government still refuses to acknowledge responsibility.

Chapter XX
My Early History

We are influenced to a large extent by the ideas we were exposed to as children. My parents were, for much of their lives immersed in the labor movement's struggles in the first half of the 20th century. My father, George Powers, fought in the Russian Revolution as a teenager and was proud of his Bolshevik background. In 1923, he came to the US to visit his family in Duluth, Minnesota, with no intention of staying. Once in the US, however, he did settle and soon joined the American Communist Party. George spent several decades as a labor union organizer in the eastern states. He had two sons by his first wife, one of whom, Bill, at the age of 82, is still an activist in California and until 2008, was president of the State Pharmaceutical Board for five years, advocating for consumers' rights. Later, George met my mother who was also involved in the Party, and they married and raised two sons. My Mom, Joan, was an artist who did many of the murals for Party activities. Later she specialized in portraits of historical figures and children.

My Dad became disillusioned with the leadership of the American Communist Party when it supported the non-aggression pact between the Soviet Union and Nazi Germany before the outbreak of World War II. He eventually left the Party, though that wasn't enough for the FBI during the McCarthy era. George was a no-show when called to testify by the House Un-American Activities Committee and was blacklisted during the 50s, unable to hold office in any labor union. He continued to be involved in union organizing without party affiliation and would often be the campaign manager for those who ran for union office even though he was banned from holding office himself.

In the late 50s, focusing more on civil rights, George founded the Frank London Brown Negro History club in Chicago with the mission of including the contributions of black Americans in the history books in the Chicago Public School system. Though self-educated, George was a charismatic speaker who immersed himself in black history. He gave lectures on that subject in high schools in the Chicago area. In the early 60s, a group of young blacks joined the club and decided there was no place for a white person teaching black history. George was drummed out of the club which soon folded because none of the new members was willing to do any work. It was one of my dad's toughest moments. His legacy was that the Board of Education did change the textbooks to include the contributions of black Americans.

As a child growing up in the home of committed leftists, I had no religious education. At the age of eight, my public school teacher would have each member of the class stand up on Monday morning and tell the rest of the class what church they had attended. I was the only one who didn't. I soon asked my little girlfriend if I could go to church with her, and for the next five years, I rarely missed a Sunday school session, fortified with a comic book or TV guide hidden in the hymnal. Finally, when I was 13, my Sunday school teacher escorted me out of the church when I contradicted his contention that the Russians couldn't have sent up the Sputnik satellite because the Bible said that man couldn't leave the earth. I never again returned to church.

I didn't appreciate my father until I was much older. His involvement in his causes left little time for bonding with his sons. He couldn't catch a ball, knew nothing of sports, and only attended three of my swim meets in 10 years. I always felt that he was disappointed that I became a coach, which he considered to be a frivolous profession. It took years for me to recognize that he was an unusual person in that he was committed to his ideals and sacrificed so much in terms of personal enjoyment in order to help others. My parents never tried to involve me in their political activities. I tagged along occasionally at rallies for various causes but only because they didn't want to leave me alone at home.

George fought a losing battle with cancer for 15 years but he didn't let it get him down. He was always out of the hospital after each operation and back home long before the doctors would allow his release.

We grew up on the far south side of Chicago, a racist all-white neighborhood known as the East Side, just off the Calumet Park beach. All beaches were segregated in Chicago in the 50s and race riots were a normal summer activity. My first taste of racism occurred when I was 11. Returning from the beach on a Sunday afternoon, we were stuck in heavy traffic which included many cars full of black families on their way back to their homes in Gary, Indiana after enjoying the Chicago beaches on the weekend. As they drove through the East Side, gangs of white youths with bricks and bats would wait for the traffic to get bogged down, and then attack the cars of the black families.

My Mom threw me on the floor as the car in front of us was attacked. When the light turned green and traffic moved on, we drove about three blocks until we passed the local police precinct. I will never forget the sight: a dozen smashed cars with bleeding black men, women and children pleading for help from the white policemen who sat on their chairs leaning back against the station as if nothing was going on.

We lived on the 3rd floor of a three-story building on the East Side. One evening, my Dad, who at that time was a steelworker at Republic Steel Corporation, brought a black co-worker home for dinner. The next night, a brick was thrown through our living room window by one of our neighbors. Another memorable event was later in the early 60's when we attended a rally at Soldiers Field in Chicago for Martin Luther King who had just been released from jail in Selma, Alabama. It was the most emotional event I have ever witnessed—around 100,000 people, mostly black, with hardly a dry eye among them, cheering as Martin Luther King entered the stadium in a convertible.

We eventually moved out of the East Side to another neighborhood called South Shore which, like much of the inner city, was rapidly transforming from all-white to all-black, as the whites fled to the suburbs. My Dad became very involved in a community drive to maintain a racially-mixed neighborhood. During that period, the local real estate agencies would hire young black thugs to terrorize the white home owners, forcing them to sell their homes at a loss which they would resell to the incoming middle class black families at a substantial profit.

Two days after leaving the hospital for the removal of a cancerous kidney, my Dad had just entered the foyer of our apartment building when he noticed a young black man following him. As George, in his weakened condition, tried to close the door, the black guy shoved it open and shot him in the face. He was turning his head as the shot was fired, and the bullet entered one cheek, took part of his tongue and a couple of teeth and exited out the other cheek. He was lucky to survive. The incident was a rude wake-up call and my parents soon moved to a safer neighborhood. Within weeks, the remaining white families had sold their homes.

A year before my Dad succumbed to the cancer that had been eating away at his body for so long, I met up with my parents in Florida, near Tampa, where they were on their last vacation together. We spent a few days at the home of my Mom's sister-in-law. The day I left, driving the car of an uncle who was also visiting from Miami, my Dad stood by the car window to say good-bye. He looked at me with such love in his eyes, but neither he nor I was able to express what we were feeling and he just said the "Have a safe trip" line.

A month later, at my new job in Sao Paulo, Brazil, I dropped a tab of acid and while listening to some music, I suddenly saw my Dad's face appear in my mind just as he looked standing by the car that last time. I just sat there and cried, so angry at myself that I had been unable to say anything meaningful to him. Finally, I wrote him a letter telling him how much I loved him and how I appreciated all the wonderful things he had done for others during his life without asking anything back. He received the letter shortly before he died and he wrote me back a letter I will always treasure.

Epilogue

I consider myself to be very fortunate. My parents passed on to me their atheism and their reliance on what is real and tangible, as well as a concern and understanding for the less fortunate. I have devoted my working years to coaching swimmers, at the same time educating those young people how to be independent and face the realities of the world. I never married nor had children but I have spent time with many wonderful women and I have a slew of swimmers who are my family in all the countries where I have resided. Recently, one of my swimmers, Pedro Cruz, who was briefly on my Venezuelan team in 1968, found me on Facebook and sent me this message:

"Dear Richard,

"What a joy to hear from you after so long without contact. In spite of the fact that our time together was short, I can never forget you because my memories of that time are so clear. My most detailed memory is of the time in Maracaibo for the National Championships in 1968 when you convinced me to train for the meet knowing there were only 12 days before my event, the 100 free. This would be my last race before I retired from swimming. I was very nervous because I hadn't trained in three months while preparing for my final exams in the university.

"I remember you had me do a workout that probably no one at that time understood. It was short and consisted almost entirely of 25 and 50 meter sprints. We arrived in Maracaibo to meet up with my rival, Jorge Volcan, who wanted more than anything else to beat me, though up to then he had never succeeded. He liked

to wage the psychological war and told me he would beat me and I would retire defeated. Your intelligent approach to the emotional factors which affected me, in spite of your lousy Spanish at that time, allowed you to understand what was going on in my mind.

I didn't realize how effective the special training you gave me was until later. The night before the prelims for my event, as I prepared to go to sleep, you came into my room and said, "Get up and get dressed. You are going out with me." Surprised, I at first refused but you finally convinced me. You took me to a bar where we drank a beer and I finally relaxed. The next day was memorable. In the prelims I lowered my time swimming in the heat just before Jorge, which I took full advantage of to give him back some of his own medicine, letting him know that he better be ready for finals because I would go much faster. That night, I swam a lifetime best and was crowned national champion, retiring with glory but never forgetting the lesson you taught me about the enormous power of the mind which permits human beings to reach the goals they strive for using will power and dedication.

"From that day, you have never left me because I always put into action what you taught me and that has allowed me to reach many other goals that I value, especially in the area of human relations.

"In me you have a friend who remembers you with affection, Pedro Cruz."

From the other end of the swimming spectrum, I received this letter from one of my masters swimmers in Davis, CA when I retired in 2008:

"Hello Coach Rick,

"I received the email regarding your plans to retire from active coaching and be a consultant to the Philippine National Swim Team, and I wanted to extend my congratulations as you begin this next chapter of your life, and also briefly just let you know how much I have appreciated your coaching here at DAM.

"I joined DAM nearly three years ago, in early summer of 05, as an injured runner looking to find an alternate way to get some exercise. I have to admit that I joined somewhat reluctantly and without any great expectations. I had done lap swimming on my own previously, and had not enjoyed it much at all, to say the least. My only swim experience had come from summers spent splashing around at the Rec Pool as a child, trying to escape the Davis heat. I'd never taken any formal swim lessons, as I had learned to stay afloat well enough to enjoy hanging out in a pool; and in high school and college, competed on the track and cross-country teams so I'd never seen a need to become more skilled in swim strokes. Therefore, my first workout

at DAM felt something like water torture, and the instructions on the whiteboard looked like a foreign language. But, I came away feeling like I'd had an amazingly good workout and intrigued enough to give it another go.

"As I persisted, you took the time to explain what some of these foreign terms like IM, LPS and 'interval' meant, I learned that four laps equaled 100 yards (or is it meters? I'm still not sure of that one), and you walked me through the various strokes, telling me to sweep the salad bowl with my arms in breaststroke, explaining to me that the backstroke was not just a mad pinwheel of arms going round and round, and attempted to teach me the butterfly, although we're still working on that one. As I became gradually more comfortable in the water, I moved on to learning flip turns, and before I knew it, I'd moved out of lane 1 and began making friends with the lane 2 and 3 swimmers. The early fall saw me occasionally sliding into lane 4, where I spent my first winter as a swimmer. I have a vivid memory of the excitement of my first time swimming in the rain and chuckled at how crazy I'd become to hop in a pool when it was near freezing outside. When I became pregnant with my third child, I appreciated the pool in a new way, enjoying the weightlessness I felt in the water and pleasantly surprised that in spite of my growing belly I could still get in a good workout.

"After the baby, I counted the days until my doctor gave me the okay to get back in the pool, and your coaching encouraged me to push myself to a new level. I came to almost enjoy the challenge of a timed set and before I knew it, I'd moved up to lane 5 and dropped 20 seconds off my LPS. Then we had one last addition to our family and I had to ease off on the intensity of my swimming for another nine months. As I've been getting back in shape after this last pregnancy, both your understanding and encouragement to not slack off have given me a real excitement to see what new levels I can reach and new skills I can learn as I look forward to a lifetime of swimming without any more 'baby breaks'.

"Your coaching has completely changed my perspective on swimming, so that I can now say that even if I have the opportunity to run again someday, I no longer will be only a runner. Swimming has now become so enjoyable and such a great part of my life, that as long as I'm able, I'll always be a swimmer now too. Thank you for taking the time to turn me into a swimmer. Your coaching is something I'll always appreciate and remember. Best wishes on your success in the Philippines. Jenny

Such feedback from my swimmers never fails to warm my heart. In spite of the dirty politics so common in the sports world, in spite of the cynicism that develops from seeing the world as it is—people of every religion killing each other in the name of God, massacring each other because of tribal or ethnic differences—knowing that I have managed to touch the lives of many of the swimmers I have coached in a positive way leaves me with a great sense of satisfaction and peace of mind.

###